# MANAGING

# SPECIAL
# COLLECTIONS

## A.M. SCHAM

D1445562

*Neal-Schuman Publishers, Inc.*
*New York     London*

*To my daughters, Sarah and Emma*

Published by Neal-Schuman Publishers, Inc.
23 Leonard Street
New York, NY 10013

**Library of Congress Cataloging-in-Publication Data**

Scham, A. M.
    Managing special collections.

    Bibliography: p.
    Includes index.
    1. Libraries—Special collections.  2. Libraries, Special—Administration.  I. Title.
Z688.A2S33   1986        026        86-16431
ISBN 0-918212-98-7

"Si l'on veut me séduire,
on n'a qu'à m'offrir des livres."

*Séguier*

# Contents

# Acknowledgments

I should like to thank the following for their help and cooperation during the preparation of this book: Professors R. S. Almagno, O.F.M., and Ellen Detlefsen, both of the University of Pittsburgh; Charles Aston, Jr., Coordinator of Special Collections at the Hillman Library; Bernadette G. Callery, head of the library of the Hunt Institute for Botanical Documentation, and Jean Gunner, in charge of the Hunt Institute's conservation/preservation program; Roderick Cave, Professor of Librarianship at Victoria University of Wellington, New Zealand; Dr. Ralph W. Franklin, Director of the Beinecke Rare Book and Manuscript Library, as well as Rutherford D. Rogers, Director of Libraries at Yale; Eleanor M. Garvey, Curator of Printing and Graphic Arts, Houghton Library, Harvard; John H. Jenkins, Former President of the Antiquarian Booksellers Association; Paul J. Pugliese, Director of Libraries at Duquesne University; Dr. Peter Spyers-Duran, Director of Libraries of Wayne State University; Donald Anderle of the New York Public Library; Dr. Lawrence W. Towner, former President and Librarian, and Mary P. Wyly, both of the Newberry Library; and Dr. David C. Weber, Director of Libraries at Stanford University.

# Introduction

The qualities unique to special collections set this department apart from the rest of the library and frequently from the library administration as well. *Managing Special Collections* is a guide for the curator to develop and apply some of the basic administrative policies essential to the management of special collections.

The decision by libraries to replace the term "rare books" with "special collections" has been of incalculable significance to both libraries and their users. If "rare books" traditionally includes mainly old, rare, unique, and valuable works, the change and expansion of such holdings offered by the term "special collections" becomes apparent immediately. Today, under this new umbrella, not only do the traditional rare and valuable works continue to be housed here, as do older works in delicate condition requiring special attention and protection to preserve them (these often including what might be termed "national treasures" being preserved for future generations to enjoy as well), but also the collection of books, printed works, and manuscripts of a single author (e.g., the Folger Shakespeare Library in Washington, D.C., and the Thornton Wilder Collection at Yale) as well as genre collections (such as the Michael Sadler Collection of Victorian novels at UCLA, and the Darlington Collection on American history at the University of Pittsburgh).

Special collections frequently exceed these boundaries. A distinguished native son or daughter may donate his or her papers, recordings, videotapes, and books (as in the case of the Sam Levenson Collection at Brooklyn College), or a government may establish a special collection to include everything on the subject of its politics, history, and commerce, which would include both the oldest and the most recent publications, in order to maintain as complete a library as possible. A good example of this is seen in the Papua New Guinea Collection at Port Moresby.

There is nothing mysterious about the reasons for the existence of special collections. Indeed, it would be fair to say that without them in our libraries and institutions, our society would be grievously poorer. And even now, despite our efforts, great gaps exist in our knowledge about certain societies, for instance the Greek Dark Ages, or the history of Ancient Crete, or even the origins of the Basque people. We learn about human history by studying human works; neglect or destroy those works and we will have caused those who have preceded us to have lived in vain, by having made it impossible for them to hand down to us the fruits of their labor and experiences. The story of humanity is, after all, the struggle not merely for existence, but also for the continuation and development of civilization, and special collections departments and museums provide a means of protecting this heritage—the physical, intellectual, and artistic achievements of past centuries.

As obvious as all this is, it must be restated, as curators of special collections frequently have a difficult time explaining and justifying their raison d'être to their budget committees. Is it really that difficult to understand? Some classical Greek plays and historical accounts have survived two and a half millennia and longer, but twice as many have been lost. Without those few remaining works, what would we know, for instance, about Periclean Athens? Special collections providing us with the knowledge of our struggle for civilization provide therefore a distilled form of wisdom, or, as Montaigne put it, "Bookes have and containe divers pleasing qualities to those that can duly choose them." At a time in history when we are rushing forward faster and faster, the importance of maintaining and expanding special collections takes on an even greater significance, for one day the youthful generations who are running at full speed today, will have to slow down, and the protection of our written heritage will be understood and appreciated.

At the same time, it is the task of curators of special collections to make known their holdings and to attract scholars and students. Sometimes this can be done through specific university courses. You may have a fine collection of English Victorian literature which can be used by graduate students and professors in this field, or your holdings on the Reformation may provide excellent source material for a course given on Reformation history. Just as often the holdings of your library have no immediate "relevance" to courses taught, but there exist scholarly groups and societies interested in just about every subject, often in foreign countries, and it is part of the curator's task to make his or her holdings known to those scholars—by articles, books, catalogs, exhibitions, and lectures. For the curator to have an ancient tome in his or her collection is wonderful; to have splendid specimens of beautiful bindings is a source of pride and even an artistic joy, but the contents of those works constitute the most important aspect of the special collection, and to fail to make those contents known is to fail to achieve a major part of the curator's job. It is his or her privileged task to select, protect, and make known to the world those works, so that people may make use of them.

# 1

# The Acquisition Policy

With the exception of the budget, no other document is so critical to the development of a special collection as the acquisition policy, and yet far too frequently it is this document which so many libraries lack, even some renowned collections.

If the university library as a whole has an acquisition policy, stating that its mission is generally to support the curricula and research needs of the university, not so the policy for special collections. Today more than ever, with budget-minded library directors and university administrators demanding an accounting of every penny spent, it soon becomes clear that the focus—or the lack of focus—of an acquisition policy can make or break a special collection.

First, without even looking at the budget, the curator can state the goals, or at least the main interests, of the special collection. It is only after considering the department's financial resources, however, that the curator can really begin to define the dimensions of a subject. For example, does the curator want to concentrate on the entire scope of nineteenth century American political development, or limit it to foreign or national policy, or concentrate on the history of one state, or perhaps on one general subject, but within a limited time period, such as the American Civil War, or even subspecialities of that war? There are as many ways of defining a subject and collections as there are dissertation subjects for the graduate student. In short, one can tailor the parameters of one's collections by adapting them to the realities of one's budget. And of course the department of special collections will in most instances be composed of several collections frequently on disparate subjects.

It is a common misconception that excellence is achieved only by a proportionate expenditure of funds. Intelligent planning is the key to the success of a special collection; it determines whether a collection is going to be significant and distinctive, or just mediocre. That a collection is composed of one or two fields only does not necessarily mean that the library's holdings are insignificant or of limited interest. A well-planned small collection, even in a library run on a tight budget of $15,000 to 20,000, could attract worldwide interest, *if properly administered.* The Simon Silverman Phenomenology Collection at Duquesne University, which is funded privately, outside the larger library budget, is an excellent example. Although one needs a realistic basic book budget, it is not the amount of the budget but how wisely the Acquisition Policy is designed and implemented which makes the difference.

Perhaps the greatest dilemma for the curator is having to decide when to say no to a collection which is being offered to the library. The inability to say no results in the development of collections which exceeds the collections' goals and which automatically spreads the existing budget even more thinly, thereby rendering it more difficult to maintain the existing collections, or to add to them in order to do them justice.

This *over-collecting,* in too many divergent fields, beyond the reasonable capabilities of the special collections's budget, is surprisingly frequent, at medium-sized, as well as at large, well-endowed universities, such as Harvard and Yale, whose lists of collections fill entire pages. Indeed, over-collecting is a national disease,[1] yet it is not always easy to avoid, for various reasons. To take a common example, a local society is closing down and is unable to find a home for its historical transactions. If the library in question does not accept their archives, the alternative is dismantling or even destroying them. The curator is now in a moral bind of sorts. Despite the curator's protests, the Hillman Library of the University of Pittsburgh, for example, accepts numerous such collections and yet lacks sufficient funds to maintain one of its fundamental collections, the Darlington Collection, which is now open only a few hours each week. It is equivalent to overloading a lifeboat with so many people that it sinks. Then there is the collection of considerable prestige and value which the donor will give to another university, if not accepted by your library. The collection in question would do justice to any library, and a competing university would no doubt be only too pleased to accept it.

Another variation on the theme derives from political pressure from above—from the director of the library, or the university's president or chancellor, or an alumni group—more or less ordering the curator to accept a collection, or perhaps simply presenting it as a fait accompli, by having already accepted a collection that has nothing to do with the acquisition policy of your collection and which is beyond the present budget to maintain.[2] The curator may be informed that once the collection is established, the donor in question intends to give considerable funds to the library or the university, perhaps even providing funds for an entirely new wing.

These cases are not unusual, and at times the curator has no choice but to accept a collection unrelated to the acquisition policy, or one which may even be worthless to anyone other than the donor, and which will only put further strain on an already committed budget. Occasionally there are other solutions for the harassed curator, as in the case of the society's records mentioned above. The local historical society may agree to take them, if only on a temporary basis, or perhaps someone can be found who can store them privately until a solution has been found. On the other hand, the curator may simply say no and lose some historical records.

When an unusually valuable but apparently irrevelant collection is offered, the curator must consider the possibility that by accepting this donation, he or she may be able to start an important new collection of use to scholars which may attract special funding in its own right. Princeton University Special Collections, for example, provides for just such an eventuality in their Collecting Guidelines:

> Unusual gifts could well alter the collecting policy for rare books. For example, if the Library accepted a substantial collection of early printed books in Welsh or Icelandic for the rare book collections, efforts would be made to build on that strength.[3]

In the case of Princeton, academic departments would support such an unusual acquisition, and no doubt parties interested in funding such a project had previously informed university officials of their interest, in the event such an occasion arose. On the other hand, the curator may instead decide that despite the tempting offer, it would be in the best interests of the library to arrange for another library to take it. The staggering cost of maintaining even completely gratis collections has been noted by Yale University's Rutherford Rogers, who pointed out what he learned the hard way: that an acquisition worth $40,000 would eventually cost the Sterling Memorial Library $1,000,000 over a span of ten years.[4] But to return to the collection recommended to the other, competing university—the curator should bear in mind that the favor done could lead to a reciprocal relationship with that institution in the future. In short, the curator of special collections must always be ready to evaluate every situation and weigh all possibilities, know how to focus on priorities and to remain diplomatically flexible throughout the process.

In the third case—being ordered to accept a collection or having had it already accepted by a university official—there is not much one can do. Political realities must be faced, even by librarians.

Needless to say, in the long run it is in the best interests of the curator to concentrate on building the basic collections, those established as written *priorities* in the acquisition policy, and which *must be limited in number* (in order to do them justice), bearing in mind, nevertheless, the possibility of future expansion. The ultimate test of success is whether, after ten or twenty years' work, the curator has built a valuable collection for scholars and society, or one of little worth. Is it an orchid, or a jungle?

In essence, then, the curator has two deadly enemies, lack of focus and lack of definition. Without focus and definition, the library's administrator becomes confused and his or her goals nebulous. By applying the term "acquisition policy," as opposed to merely "goals and objectives," "collecting guidelines," "policy statement," and the like, we are focusing on the *acquisition* of specific collections, specific subjects. The lack of such a definitive policy will result in muddled thinking, which in turn will be reflected by the composition of the collection. Given the premise that an acquisition policy is indeed critical to the development of a special collection, we can turn to the three basic elements of such a policy: its goals (or mission), objectives, and priorities.


## GOALS OR MISSION STATEMENT

Although we have begun to discuss the subject of acquisition policies and have described some of their inherent elements, no precise definition has been given. No specific format has been suggested. Basically, the acquisition policy must state the general purpose (and even philosophy), goals, or mission of a special collection, then define its goals and objectives and finally, within the latter category, the stated priorities.[5] And yet there is no universal form followed to achieve this. Some rare book libraries, such as the Beinecke Rare Book and Manuscript Library at Yale[6] and the Hunt Institute for Botanical Documentation in Pittsburgh,[7] have no written acquisition policy at all; the matter is dealt with informally, as needs arise. But for those public and university libraries that do have policies, the varieties of presentation are considerable, though they rarely are actually referred to specifically as acquisition policies.

The University of Washington has a written "goal" supported by nine objectives. The "goal" states that the purpose is:

> to engage in planning, development, conservation, security, reference service, and supervised use of collections of rare, scarce, unique, and other specialized materials essential for advanced study and research in intellectual history, social history, literary history and art history.[8]

The Special Collections Department of Iowa State University, however, is even more succinct with one general mission and eight objectives. Its mission reads: "To collect, organize and preserve manuscripts, rare books and University archival materials."[9] The head of Stanford's Special Collections provided the philosophy for his Collection Development Policy under the surprising rubric, Programmatic Information.

> The Department of Special Collections collects, preserves and manages the use of materials which are considered rare, unique or in some other way extraordinary and therefore require special handling and use. Rare materials are intended primarily for the research needs of Stanford faculty, graduate students, and undergraduates who are conducting research that warrants use of Special Collections.[10]

Princeton's Rare Book Division's General Collecting Guidelines include its "general purpose":

> The rare book collections protect many of the most valuable, scarcest, or most important materials in the Library's collections. Because of concentrated attention paid to the collections over the years by donors and members of the library staff, the collections are quite large (about 150,000 volumes) and able to support intensive research, especially in the fields of English and American literature. Although the collections serve primarily persons affiliated with Princeton, they also support teaching, exhibitions, and research elsewhere, through loans and photographic reproductions. The

collections are used mainly by university students in art, literature and history.[11]

These formats reflect different philosophies. Of those shown, Stanford's seems closest to what the overall goal or purpose of a special collection should be. Princeton's policy statement lacks coherence and adds such extraneous matter as the number of volumes in the collection. There is no clearcut rule whether this initial statement should include the general subjects covered in the collection. The University of Washington and Princeton both do; Stanford and Iowa State University do not. As subjects should be mentioned under both Objectives and Priorities, however, they may not be required here as well.

## OBJECTIVES

Generally speaking we are referring here to administrative objectives for the collection, as opposed both to specific library materials, which will be dealt with under Priorities, and to administrative rules and regulations or procedures. But too often the objectives listed say little. For instance, the first objective of the Iowa State University Special Collections Department:[12]

> To develop efficient methods for acquiring and organizing for ready access publications, records and other archival materials of the University.

Who does not want general efficiency in acquiring and organizing materials? Their second objective is essentially valid and applies here:

> To acquire as gifts collections of manuscripts and records that fall within the Library's acquisitions scope and to organize them for ready access by researchers.

To wish to acquire donations of manuscripts within a prescribed scope is a bona fide policy objective, but the last part of the statement, "to organize them for ready access by researchers," is automatically understood, for, after all, what is a library for? Their third objective does not address the subject at hand:

To provide complete bibliographic records for the Library's rare book collections and to suggest additions to this collection.

The fourth objective, "To offer complete reference service for all materials" in the collection seems sound enough, but is a normal library service to be considered an objective or goal? Nor does objective number five belong here:

To maintain and submit to the Library Administration statistical data on new acquisitions and on growth and use of the collection.

This is a daily task of library personnel, not a long-term objective. Such data referred to here would automatically be included in the annual report. The next objective appears to be one of common sense, and should not even have to be written (unless as a requirement of new personnel):

To be informed about new techniques and methodologies that are important for preservation and organization of materials in the Department.

Surely any person in an administrative capacity is expected to remain fully informed about his or her profession! The next one also must qualify as an elementary administrative task:

To develop, maintain and continually revise written manuals for all departmental procedures.

Administrative procedures have nothing to do with the acquisition policy. The last objective—to develop "goals" on short- and long-range bases for collecting—establishes that the party drawing up these "objectives" did not understand the definition and purpose of the document under study. One draws up goals and objectives because it is sound management. To develop a goal that states that your goal is to develop goals is redundant! It would perhaps be more appropriate to state as an objective: to develop collections in certain fields, such as English and French literature, or European history. At a later stage, when adequate additional funds become available on an annual basis, to start collecting in the fields of, say, incunabula, the Florentine Renaissance, and American literary manuscripts. These general fields of subject development are, after all, elementary acquisition objectives and state immediately, and far more effectively, than that which the eighth or final objective does. These could then be refined further by the more detailed priority list.

The University of Washington's objectives duplicate those of Iowa State to a certain extent, such as providing "advanced bibliographical reference service" and soliciting gifts and encouraging donations. One objective listed obviously does not belong here:

> To shelve or otherwise store materials in whatever ways are deemed most advantageous to staff and to users. . . .

Shelving instructions are not long-term objectives of a special collection. They have also included a general objective on subject matter, and have added another to encourage the participation of faculty, students, and the public in the development of the collections.

If one were to try to sum up some of the valid objectives of an acquisition policy for special collections, they would include:

1. To encourage the donation of collections, works, and materials which fall within the collecting parameters of the department.
2. To encourage and establish endowment funds with which to support as much of the collection's budgetary needs as possible.
3. To collect materials in the following primary areas: (here name them), but consider future expansion into other areas should the conditions be such as to warrant this.
4. To produce publications pertaining to the department's collections and activities, when deemed advisable and useful.
5. To encourage the study and use of the department's collections through exhibitions, loans, photocopies and microfilm, lectures and seminars (and through the introduction of fellowships, if possible).
6. To establish exchange relationships with other special collections.

These six objectives are all short- and long-term goals and are basic enough to apply to the vast majority of libraries and collections. But this list is flexible and other points may be added according to the needs of the library. For instance, some libraries will want to work within national networks, or some may have a very unusual objective unique to their special circumstances. But it should be kept in mind that objectives for acquisition are not departmental administrative rules, regulations, or procedures. How one catalogs or shelves materials or collects data—all are out of place here.

## PRIORITIES

With the general objectives of the library's collection clearly established, the next task is to determine one's collecting priorities and to define their dimensions. Most library funds are probably used ineffectively as a result of not establishing this particular focus and then not adhering to it. Again, it is the question of wanting an orchid or a jungle. The American Library Association has long acknowledged the inherent problems and necessities here and in 1979 came out with *Guidelines for Collection Development,* which states: "Libraries should identify the long- and short-range needs of their clientele, and establish priorities for the allocation of resources to meet those needs. A collection development policy statement is an orderly expression of those priorities as they relate to the development of library resources."[13]

Priority lists can be formulated in several ways. For instance, the Newberry Library of Chicago states their priorities in three paragraphs.

    I. Within the humanities, the Library's collections have come to concentrate in the following:
      A. *Western Europe* (History, literature, and culture) from the Middle Ages through the early 19th century. In general, France, Italy and Spain are strongly represented; Germany and the Low Countries are somewhat weaker; Scandinavian and Slavic materials are not considered among the primary strengths of the library.
      B. *Great Britain:* Strong from the beginnings up into the early 20th century.
      C. *Latin America:* Strong from the beginnings up to the time of liberation from European Control.
      D. *United States & Canada:* Strong from discovery up to World War I, in certain areas of Midwestern interest, up to World War II.

This first section indicates the general areas covered only, and it is noted that certain subjects (such as France, Italy, and Spain) receive much more attention and greater funds than do others (such as Germany and the Low Countries, or Scandinavian and Slavic materials).

Next the Newberry states what the library specifically excludes and why.

> II. The Newberry does *not* collect material in the following areas: Science, medicine, and technology (in deference to the John Crerar Library and other institutions); the visual arts, except certain areas of the graphic arts (in deference to the Ryerson Library of the Art Institute of Chicago and other institutions); social science and other topics of current interest (in other specialized institutions such as the Library of International Relations); archaeology and antiquity, materials on non-western civilizations, business, finance, and economics. In any of these areas, however, specific titles may be found at the Newberry, for purposes of complementing a strong collection in another area.

Finally the policy states the top priority collections:

> III. In the following subjects, the Newberry Library attempts to maintain a definitive collection for research purposes.
> A. History of printing, typography, and calligraphy (John M. Wing Foundation).
> B. American Indian history, discovery and exploration, and related areas (Edward E. Ayer Collection).
> C. History of music (Jane Oakley Fund), including books about music and scores for study purposes, but not sound recordings.
> D. Portugese and Brazilian studies (William B. Greenlee Collection).
> E. Western Americana (Everett D. Graff Collection).
> F. Italian Renaissance, history of libraries and of bibliography, family history and heraldry, Arthuriana, courtesy books, the history of cartography, historical philology, Philippines, Utopias, voyages and travels, among others.

In these few paragraphs the Newberry has indicated what its primary interests are and which subjects are collected in depth. That library has provided a simple and useful means of establishing its basic priorities and as a result, with well over one and a quarter million volumes and thousands of manuscripts, it is an attractive center of learning.

Princeton University's Rare Book Division is only one of several special collections on that campus, and its collection of 150,000 volumes concentrates, at least theoretically, in the fields of English and

American literature. The Division's Guidelines state what is excluded (e.g., East Asian rare books and early works in Hebrew or Arabic), as well as what general areas are included. These subjects are classified in no order of priority, other than the notation that they are collected at Level 4 (the research level), as opposed to the highest, Level 5 (exhaustive).

American Civil War
American history of Colonial and Revolutionary periods
American illustrated books printed before 1870
American Indians
Angling
Arabian Nights
Books in the indigenous languages of Middle America, e.g., editions of the Popol Vuh
Early and important works in all fields of knowledge
Early voyages and travel
Emblem books
Fables
History and philosophy of science, including medicine
New Jerseyana printed before 1850
Nineteenth-century English literature, especially the pre-Raphaelites, the Victorian novelists, and the 1890's
Princeton authors
Restoration drama
Victorian bookbindings
Western Americana
Works in the language of a traditional people, e.g., Ebo, Navaho, Tagalog, Tahitian

Although the Rare Books Division maintains an exhaustive acquisition policy for four collections (William Cowper, Emily Dickinson, F. Scott Fitzgerald, and Woodrow Wilson), it does collect the works of the following at Level 4 (research level):

Thomas Bailey Aldrich
John James Audubon
Aubrey Vincent Beardsley
Sir Max Beerbohm
Richard Palmer Blackmur
William Blake
Sir Thomas Browne

George Gordon Noël Byron, 6th baron Byron
Francois Auguste René Chateaubriand
Samuel Langhorne Clemens
James Gould Cozzens
The Cruikshanks: George, Isaac Robert and Isaac

Thus, although Princeton University does attempt to establish some vague priorities, in general the subject contents listed above reflect a collection which may have lacked positive and correct focus on its stated aims (of concentrating on English and American literature). The funds deflected from the stated objectives have perhaps weakened what—although still good and interesting—could have been a far more distinctive collection. Indeed, there is a reason it is essential for all libraries to state their priorities unequivocally.

A system of priorities is necessary for any library or special collection. Priorities can be ranked in order of importance—1,2,3—or A,B,C—and a system of "levels of collection" can be drawn up. As seen in these examples, once priorities are ranked, the levels of collection development must be defined and applied. The American Library Association has come out with formal definitions of five collection levels which have already been accepted by many libraries across the country. The five levels include: A. Comprehensive Level; B. Research Level; C. Study Level; D. Basic Level; and E. Minimal Level. Theoretically, it is Level A, the comprehensive level alone, which concerns us and which is defined by the ALA as:

> A collection which a library endeavors, so far as is reasonably possible, to include all significiant works of recorded knowledge (publications, manuscripts, other forms) for a necessarily defined field. This level of collecting intensity is that which maintains a "special collection"; the aim, if not the achievement, is exhaustiveness.[14]

As we are not always in a position to afford to maintain an exhaustive collection on a subject, it is useful to note the next two lower levels: Level B, the research level

> includes the major published source materials required for dissertations and independent research, including materials containing research reporting, new findings, scientific experimental results, and other information useful to researchers. It also includes all important reference works and a wide

selection of specialized monographs, as well as an extensive collection of journals and major indexing and abstracting services in the field.[15]

Level C, or study level, as defined by the ALA refers to

> a collection which supports undergraduate or graduate course work, or sustained independent study; that is, which is adequate to maintain knowledge of a subject required for limited or generalized purposes, of less than research intensity. It includes a wide range of basic monographs, complete collections of the works of important writers, selections from the works of secondary writers, a selection of representative journals, and the reference tools and fundamental bibliographical apparatus pertaining to the subject.[16]

Scholars involved in serious research on a subject, say in the humanities, are really concerned only with the Comprehensive Level, Level A, for they require access not only to exhaustive collections of published works, but also to collections which provide primary sources, i.e., original sources of information, from which all other sources, such as published works, are taken. If this is a music collection, this might be original handwritten manuscripts prepared by Bach or Beethoven, or in a historical collection, perhaps a prime minister's handwritten notes and documents. The librarian must ever bear in mind that the collection with which he or she is concerned is collected for the use of scholars, not for the librarian. It is collected to fill a specific need within a specific field of study.

Thus, a special collection at the highest level, maintained for special use, must attempt to collect everything possible on a subject, whether in a fine binding or badly in need of repair. To be sure, no single collection anywhere can truly be exhaustive, for however wonderful and seemingly complete a collection is, there are always works which cannot be found or are unknown or, as frequently occurs, some important books or manuscripts on the subject are in other special collections and archives. A good example of this is in the collections of the correspondence and manuscripts of French novelist Emile Zola. Most of them are in the Fonds des Manuscrits of the Bibliothèque Nationale in Paris, but other documents and correspondence are in archives in Aix, in the Taylor Library in Oxford, and in the Houghton Library at Harvard. However, the purpose at Level A is always to maintain as exhaustive a collection as possible.

## OTHER MEANS OF DEFINING THE COLLECTION

Most libraries contain either one general special collections department, with special subcollections, or else several different special collections scattered across a campus, throughout their library system, and in some cases there appear to be combinations of both—one large rare book library, for example, and several bibliographers in charge of separate specialized collections elsewhere in the library system. Regardless of the organization applied, libraries frequently establish collecting guidelines defining their restriction. Such categories include subject matter, languages collected or excluded, chronological limits, geographical restrictions, and types of materials to be collected or excluded. Princeton's Rare Book Division once again affords a good example:

> D. Languages collected and excluded.
>> Collected: English, French, German, Latin, Italian, Greek, Spanish, Portuguese, Scandinavian languages, native American languages.
>> Excluded: Except for Chinese, Japanese and Korean (which are collected by the Gest Oriental Library), no language is theoretically excluded from the collections.
> E. Geographical Limits.
>> There are no geographical limits to the collection, except as implied above in D.
> F. Chronological limits.
>> Theoretically there are no chronological limits to the collection.
> G. Types of material collected and excluded.
>> Collected: monographs; serials; pamphlets; ephemera.
>> Excluded: audiovisual materials.

The chronological limitations discussed above are fairly common throughout special collections in the United States. Stanford, for instance, in addition to following most of the limiting divisions mentioned at Princeton, has the following:

Chronological:
> A. Rare Book Collection: From the invention of printing (block books) to modern times, with less interest in pre-1456 imprints. In practice, there is an emphasis on 16th century continental books, 18th century British imprints, early American titles and Latin American titles printed before 1825.

Princeton follows these limitations (though the policy quoted above, under F, would indicate there are none):

a. 1801 in Continental Europe, in England and in English abroad.
b. 1821 in the United States east of the Mississippi, in Canada, South America and Central America.
c. 1826 in Eastern Europe.
d. 1876 in the United States west of the Mississippi.
e. 1901 in Africa and the Pacific.

The University of Washington, however, established the following chronological guidelines:

Books, etc., printed in Continental Europe before 1650, books printed in England before 1750, books printed in the Americas before 1850, and any books of later date that are recognized as rare, scarce, extremely fragile. . . .

The Newberry, on the other hand, approaches the problems with the following constraints.

American history and literature to 1900
Art of war before 1890
Continental Renaissance to 1600
English history and literature to 1900 (includes fiction before 1740 and imprints to 1800)
English and American periodicals before 1900
European history to 1800
History of philology to 1900
Latin American history and literature to 1820
19th century socialism and communism

We have now seen the absolute necessity for the preparation of an acquisition policy, and how critical such a policy is to the development of any library or special collection. Although it may be of any length, this document should be as clear and simple as possible. The purpose of the acquisition policy is to remind the curator and the staff, that they must define the collection through their acquisitions or else pay the price and allow it to fall into mayhem. Finally, it should be kept in mind that the Acquisition Policy is meant to assist in the *acquisition* of materials; it is not meant to provide administrative rules and procedures.

## References

1. Over-collecting does not necessarily imply a large number of collections. For example, the Brooklyn College Library has recently acquired the Sam Levenson Collection—composed chiefly of correspondence, manuscripts, and recordings of broadcasts—but with no increase in the budget and no private endowment to allow for it to be cataloged, maintained, and preserved. Indeed the materials have not even been placed in a special room with air-conditioning and humidity control, nor are there plans for this.
2. See Chapter 7 on Gifts and Exchanges. Administrators going over the curator's head on occasion not only accept such a collection, but accept some serious financial responsibilities on the part of the curator, such as providing a special room and library staff for the collection, or the promise not to break up or dispose of any of it (even if the library has duplicates of much of it). The funding sometimes provided by donors for the upkeep of their collections usually does not go very far.
3. Princeton University's Acquisition Policies, Rare Book Division, quoted in *Special Collections Kit 57,* p. 53-2, published by the Systems and Procedures Exchange Center, Association of Research Libraries, Office of Management Studies, in Washington, D.C., September 1979. Hereafter these publications will be cited as SPEC Kit X.
4. Rutherford D. Rogers and David C. Webster, *University Library Administration* (New York: H. W. Wilson, 1971), p. 114.
5. On the subject of acquisition policy and establishing goals, objectives, and priorities, see: Elizabeth Futas, ed., *Library Acquisition Policies and Procedures,* Second Edition, A Neal-Schuman Professional Book (Phoenix: Oryx Press, 1984). The author has provided a series of documents from a variety of colleges and public libraries across the country under three divisions: Academic Library Policies, Public Library Policies, and Partial Library Policies by Category. On the other hand, William A. Katz, in his work, *Collection Development: The Selection of Materials for Libraries* (New York: Holt, Rinehart and Winston, 1980) does indeed briefly address the issue of drafting these basic documents, in the first chapter under "Selection Objectives and Goals," and "Collection Development Policy Statement," but he does not attempt to deal with special collections. See p. 12 ff. See also, Bonnie Good Buzzell's and Rosemary L. Cullen's "Special Collections, Small Presses, and Gathering Plans," which touches upon acquisitions for the Harris Collection of Brown University, included as a chapter in Peter Spyers-Duran's and Thomas Mann Jr's *Shaping Library Collections for the 1980s* (Phoenix: Oryx Press, 1980).
6. Ralph W. Franklin, Director of the Beinecke, to the author, February 1, 1893.
7. Interview with the Librarian of the Hunt Institute, Bernadette Callery, January 1983.

8. SPEC Kit 57, p.6.
9. This policy is dated November 1974.
10. Collection Development Policy, by Florian J. Shasky, Principal Biblio-
    grapher, Stanford University, dated July 6, 1978. Compare with E.
    Coulouma, and C. Peligry, "Le fonds ancien de la Bibliothèque Municipal
    de Toulouse," *Bulletin des Bibliothèques de France,* 27 (December 1982),
    pp. 699-705.
11. SPEC Kit 57, p. 53-1.
12. In addition to the objectives discussed hereafter, see those quoted by Eliz-
    abeth Futas, *Library Acquisition Policies and Procedures* for the Sterling
    C. Evans Library of Texas A & M University, for the Library of the Uni-
    versity of Wisconsin-Stout, the University of Detroit, Eastern Illinois Un-
    iversity Library, the Klinck Memorial Library of Concordia College,
    etc.
13. See David L. Perks, Editor, *Guidelines for Collection Development*
    (Chicago: American Library Association, 1979), p. 5.
14. *Ibid.* p. 3.
15. *Ibid.*
16. *Ibid.,* pp. 3-4.

# 2

# The Budget

## SOME APPROACHES TO BUDGETING

For the special collections department, either in a public or a university library, the assignment of a budget appears to be the lowest priority of the library administration, mainly because a specific rationale for its existence is not always apparent, in terms of practical everyday realities. Indeed, as noted in the preceding chapter, special collections in some smaller universities and colleges are allocated no regular budget at all. Some departments are neither consulted about their budgetary needs nor are they even expected to submit a regular budget request. The curator may simply send in a note suggesting a total sum for acquisitions and another figure for supplies. Such a "system" on the part of the library administration is utterly out of place in twentieth century library management. How can an accountant in a business office possibly know the needs of a rare books and manuscripts library? The vast majority of university libraries still follow this unfortunate policy.

When budgets do exist, however, they fall into various categories and include the following: the line-item budget, the lump sum budget, the formula budget, the program budget, the performance budget, the planning, programming, and budgeting system (PPBS), and the zero-base budget (ZBB). The next question is obvious: which budgetary system best fits the needs of special collections?

The line-item budget takes a general subject line for each component of the library's entire budget, such as salaries, wages, telephone service, travel, institutional supplies, etc., lumping everything from

## FIGURE 1   Line-Item Budget Summary Sheet[1]

SUMMARY

Department or Program:  Library

Department No.: 0153

For Fiscal Year: 1986-87

| Control No. | Expenditures | Actual Prior Year 1984-85 | Budget Current Year 1985-86 | Budget Request Next Year 1986-87 | Budget Approved Next Year 1986-87 |
|---|---|---|---|---|---|
| 100 | Salaries | 141,000 | 142,000 | 153,000 | |
| 102 | Wages | 14,000 | 14,500 | 18,000 | |
| 103 | Staff benefits | 23,000 | 23,200 | 25,500 | |
| 108 | Contracted Services | 6,500 | 6,800 | 7,500 | |
| 109 | Telephone Service | 8,700 | 8,900 | 9,000 | |
| 111 | Office Equipment | 4,000 | 4,300 | 4,200 | |
| 112 | Office Supplies | 10,000 | 11,200 | 12,000 | |
| 113 | Travel | 5,000 | 5,000 | 5,000 | |
| 114 | Instructional Supplies | 93,000 | 96,000 | 100,000 | |
| | TOTAL | $305,200 | $311,900 | $334,200 | |

every department of the library falling into that general category into Figure 1 for such a summary sheet. Obviously this form leaves much to be desired, as it avoids the specific requirements of each department and thereby skirts this entire planning process. The lump sum budget, on the other hand, is now extremely rare. It assigns a single sum to the library's director to use as he or she deems fit. The formula budget (and there are several formulas) is fairly popular in university circles, though not nearly so much as the line-item. When the Association of Research Libraries prepared its questionnaires for the 1977 SPEC Kit on the preparation of the library budget, sixty-eight libraries replied to their queries, and of that number, forty (58%) confirmed that they were using the line-item budget, whereas only three libraries were actually submitting some form of formula, performance, or zero-base budget to their parent institution. For their own internal use seventeen libraries indicated that they were changing from a line-item budget to a program or ZBB, while two others which had been using the programmatic approach had decided to revert to the line-item.[2] Libraries—whether public or private—are still in search of the ideal budgetary instrument.

The planning, programming, and budgeting system was introduced to the United States Defense Department by Robert McNamara in 1963, and President Lyndon Johnson extended this concept to all federal agencies within the next couple of years, the system soon spreading to many state governments as well. PPBS had its strong advocates, such as Harry Williams, who declared,

> The basic principle of program budgeting is to derive and structure an annual budget in such a way that it reflects the annual portion of all the major programs in a university which, in turn, promote the over all purposes and objectives of that institution.[3]

And James Farmer stressed the two-phase decision process in PPBS, planning and programming, and emphasized that budgeting was intended to implement and control, but not to be used to make basic decisions. He stressed instead that the planning phase required the preparation of objectives of the institution concerned, "the development of alternative courses of action, and an analysis of these alternatives."[4] Since then numerous articles have been published on both PPBS and ZBB, but what the proponents of PPBS have not pointed out is that its implementation, though providing a far better understanding of the workings of their institutions, does not automatically mean appreciable savings, nor do they stress sufficiently at PPBS depends on vast amounts of statistics concerning the cost-effectiveness of various programs. And though there are those who support PPBS in university systems, Guy De Genaro points out that it results in ever more insurmountable problems, not the least of which is that of providing the right series of objectives.[5] And the idea of converting library staff to developing a massive statistical collating network is not appealing. In the long run, as Spyers-Duran rightly concluded, would the greatly increased expense necessary for data collection and analysis really justify the final product?[6]

Zero-based budgeting (see Figure 2) has aroused even more controversy. Articles by Elise Hayton, Rodney M. Hersberger, and Ann G. Sarndal all address the issue of ZBB. Elise Hayton, of McMaster University finally came to the conclusion that the great amount of work required in the process by library personnel was not justified as the library's budget remained unchanged.[7] Rodney Hersberger points out that the university system as a whole had to follow ZBB or it could not be applied at all.[8] Anne G. Sarndal was much more specific in her criticisms, although she concluded that though ZBB was time-consuming, when done seriously "it is probably worthwhile," again not because it guarantees great savings, but because it fosters a better understanding of the organization, its objectives, and how best to achieve them.[9] ZBB requires the following steps: (1) development of planning assumptions, (2) identification of decision units, (3) analysis of each decision unit, (4) ranking of various activities and movements according to priority, and the presentation of alternative methods, (5) the preparation of a budget at various levels, and finally (6) performance evaluation of all these throughout the library. As Sarndal points out, the failings are many: planning results have not generally been linked to individual units to show implications; considerable difficulties have arisen over identifying decision units in the first place; some department managers have simply refused to give the time and attention needed to look at the decisions and possible alternatives; and the whole concept of ranking is fraught with problems, frequently involving petty departmental feuds. Figure 2 provides an abbreviated ZBB Form that may be applied to some libraries.[10]

If PPBS could not easily be applied to a special collection, nor could a standard zero-base budgeting format, then what about formulas? The American Library Association promoted some general formulas many years ago,[11] such as advocating that the total library budget equal five percent of the total university budget, but the formulas that were really needed to pinpoint managerial and administrative problems and to develop blueprints over the next several years were prepared independently of the ALA and grew incredibly complex. Frequently they ended up as controversial political tools in the hands of the advocates fostering special interest groups on campuses (e.g.,

## FIGURE 2   Zero-Base Budgeting Form

Prepared by:
Date:

| Program Name: | Priority Rank: |
|---|---|
| Department: | Level: |

Statement of Purpose (goals and objectives):

Description of Activity:

Benefits/Desired Results:

Alternatives/Other Options (to achieve same or partial results):

Consequences If Activity Is Not Approved/Is Eliminated:

| Costs/Resources Required | Prior Period | Budgeted Period |
|---|---|---|
| Personnel:<br>  Professional<br>  Para-professional<br>  Hourly Wages<br>  Secretarial Staff<br>Operations:<br>  Supplies<br>  Equipment<br>  Travel<br>  Contracted Services<br>  Other | | |
| Total: | | |

Approved by:
Title: Director of the Library
Date:

science versus humanities). Various state universities came out with their own intricate systems, sometimes based on the Clapp-Jordan Model[12] or those introduced by the University of California, by Alabama, Florida, Ohio, Wisconsin, and Washington, all of which introduced a complete or partial formula program for staffing, allocating funds, materials, etc. But the formulas used have either become so complex that only "specialists" in the narrow realm know what is being talked about, or else, even when the formulas are reduced to their simplest components, as in the following example in Figure 3 prepared by Spyers-Duran, it becomes obvious that they simply are not at all relevant to special collections.[13]

Nevertheless, the fact remains that these systems simply do not apply to special collections. They are established for the most part on ratios based on the number of graduate programs, graduate students, and professors using the libraries, the number of books allowed for professor and student, the number and types of degrees given in each field, the number of grants and amount of money budgeted in each area, etc. As we have seen, the varieties of approach to the allocation of library resources do not meet the problems posed by special collections. The very uniqueness and the quality of those materials refute any attempt at quantitative application—e.g., application to number of professors and graduate students using so many manuscript letters, or the graduate degrees issued in such fields—and such attempts are meaningless.

Although the general line-item budget and the use of nebulous rubrics lacking specific analysis make it easier for the library director to present a general budget, most special collections can nevertheless prepare—if only for their own internal use, and then later convert to the line-item—a program budget. And yet a large number of special collections do not make a serious attempt at preparing a detailed budget of any kind. The variety of program budgets is limited only by the curator's imagination and needs, and many of these are essentially a combination of zero-base budgets and programmatic approaches, which means that the curator is providing a strict account of every penny spent. For example, a very simple program budget might look like the one in Figure 4. It is tailor-made to fit the specific needs of a special collection, and thus the curator is free to add some special item if necessary. These results can then be prepared with previous programmatic budgets.

FIGURE 3 Components of Materials Formulas

| CALIFORNIA | FLORIDA | WASHINGTON | UPPER DIV. UNIV. LIBS. |
|---|---|---|---|
| | | | **Part A: Books** |
| 1. Basic collection = 75,000 vols. for first 600 FTE students | 1. No. doctoral programs × 15,000 volumes | 1. No. doctoral programs × 24,500 volumes | 1. No. doctoral programs × 21,800 volumes |
| 2. Add 10,000 vols. for each add'l 200 FTE students | 2. No. masters programs w/o doct. × 7,500 vols | 2. No. masters programs w/o doct. × 6,100 vols | 2. No. masters programs w/o doct. × 10,500 vols. |
| 3. Add 3,000 vols. for each masters program | 3. No. masters programs with doctoral × none | 3. No. masters programs with doctoral × 3,050 | 3. No. masters programs with doctoral × none |
| 4. Add 5,000 vols. for each doctoral program | 4. No. FTE faculty × 100 volumes | 4. No. FTE faculty × 100 volumes | 4. No. FTE faculty × 115 volumes |
| 5. Total volumes *Generated* | 5. No. FTE students × 15 volumes | 5. No. FTE students × 15 volumes | 5. No. FTE students × 18 volumes |
| 6. No. volumes *in collection* | 6. Basic collection = 85,000 volumes | 6. Basic collection = 85,000 volumes | 6. Basic collection = 100,000 volumes |
| 7. Collection deficiency or (over minimum) | 7. Total vols. *generated* | 7. Total vols. *generated* | 7. Total vols. *generated* |
| | 8. No. vols. *in collection* | 8. No. vols. *in collection* | 8. No. vols. *in collection* |
| | 9. Collection deficiency or (over minimum) | 9. Collection deficiency or (over minimum) | 9. Collection deficiency or (over minimum) |
| | | | **Part B: Periodicals/Serials** |
| | | | 1. Basic collection of 1,000 subscriptions (Titles) |
| | | | *Plus* |
| | | | 2. 10 titles per FTE faculty |
| | | | 3. 5 titles per MA w/o doct. |
| | | | 4. 3 titles per MA w/o doct. |
| | | | 5. 15 titles per doctoral |
| | | | 6. Total subscriptions (Titles) |

As the data are as complete as possible, the curator can take whatever information is required and transfer it to the line-item budget for the library director. Figure 4 includes only amounts for conservation/preservation and acquisitions, but the other categories would be completed in a similar fashion. On the other hand, should the director or budget office require a simple zero-base budgeting form, a modification of the example in Figure 2 can be used.

## THE FIVE-YEAR PROGRAM PRIORITY BUDGET

Assuming that the program budget fits the needs of special collections, this can work effectively only when the collection's objectives and goals are listed, and that is why it is necessary for the acquisition policy to reduce them to the form of specific priorities. Thus by knowing that we want to apply a programmatic budget based on the prioriteis which have been established in the acquisition policy, the curator can feel that he or she is on very solid ground when beginning this task. I have provided examples in this chapter employing four priorities only. It behooves the curators of special collections to try to employ the simplest and most effective system.

The rare book library in Figure 5 consists of two sections: a general collections area, to which is applied the regular budget but including the unrestricted gifts and donations, and the individual special collections, that is, those supported by restricted, endowed funds. It will be noted that the main difference between the general collection and the endowed special collection in this respect is that each of the endowed collections automatically has a number-one priority, notwithstanding the necessity of establishing sub-priorities within each special collection, of course; whereas each of the main areas of the general collection is not automatically assured X-dollars unless the acquisition policy assigns each a number-one priority. This system is fairly common in large rare book libraries whether at Harvard, Yale, or the Newberry. The following examples have been created for demonstration only, however, and therefore do not apply to any specific existing library or institution. A worksheet would be made for each of the special collections in order to help define the budgetary needs, as in Figure 5, in which priority numbers are planned.

Each of the columns of priority numbers listed to the right of the subject (in Figure 5) naturally reflects a totally separate acquisition policy, the three separate budgets listed together here solely for pur-

## FIGURE 4  Internal Program Budget for Special Collections

| | | Budget Request 1986-87 | Next Year's Approved Budget 1986-87 |
|---|---|---|---|
| PERSONNEL: | 1 Director | | |
| | 2 Curators | | |
| | 2 Reference Librarians | | |
| | 2 Catáloguers | | |
| | 1 Conservator | | |
| | 2 Secretaries | | |
| | 6 Students | | |
| STAFF BENEFITS | | | |
| CONTRACTED SERVICES | | | |
| INSURANCE | | | |
| TELEPHONE SERVICES & COMPUTERS | | | |
| OFFICE EQUIPMENT | | | |
| OFFICE SUPPLIES | | | |
| PHOTOCOPYING | | | |
| TRAVEL | | | |
| EXHIBITIONS: | 1. Photography | | |
| | 2. Special Supplies | | |
| | 3. Printed Brochures | | |
| | 4. Advertising | | |
| | 5. Entertainment | | |
| CONSERVATION/PRESERVATION: | | | |
| | 1. Binding | $ 10,000 | |
| | 2. Materials | 8,000 | |
| | 3. Microforms | 3,000 | |
| TOTAL C/P: | | $21,000  $21,000 | $21,000 |
| | | 6,000 | |

```
ACQUISITIONS:

      1. Bibliographical.
      2. General Collections.
            a. Books            18,000
            b. Manuscripts       5,000
            c. Serials           2,000         25,000

      3. Endowed Foundations.
            a. Foundation A
                  1) Books      13,000
                  2) Manuscripts     0        $13,000

            b. Foundation B
                  1) Books      15,000
                  2) Manuscripts 11,000        26,000

            c. Foundation C
                  1) Books       8,000
                  2) Manuscripts 15,000        23,000
                                               62,000

                     TOTAL ACQUISITIONS       $93,000


TOTAL BUDGET REQUESTED                                  $93,000        $93,000
```

## FIGURE 5  Priority Numbers

| | | P.N. | P.N. | P.N. |
|---|---|---|---|---|
| I. | General European Collection. | | | |
| A. | France: | | | |
| | 1. History till 1815 | I | I | I |
| | 2. Literature till 1815 | II | I | I |
| | 3. Philosophy till 1815 | III | I | III |
| | 4. Science till 1815 | IV | I | IV |
| B. | Great Britain: | | | |
| | 1. History till 1815 | I | III | I |
| | 2. Literature till 1815 | II | III | I |
| | 3. Philosophy till 1815 | III | III | III |
| | 4. Science till 1815 | IV | III | IV |
| C. | Spain: | | | |
| | 1. History till 1815 | I | II | II |
| | 2. Literature till 1815 | II | II | II |
| | 3. Philosophy till 1815 | III | II | III |
| | 4. Science till 1815 | IV | II | IV |
| II. | Special, Endowed Collections. | | | |
| A. | The A Foundation, Danish Literature. | | | |
| | 1. Medieval | III | II | I |
| | 2. 1400-1648 | II | I | I |
| | 3. 1649-1900 | I | III | I |
| B. | The B Foundation, American Indians. | | | |
| | 1. North American | I | III | II |
| | 2. Central American | II | II | III |
| | 3. South American | III | I | I |
| C. | The C Foundation, Florentine Renaissance. | | | |
| | 1. Art | I | II | I |
| | 2. Literature | II | I | II |
| | 3. Medicine | III | III | III |

Each column of priority numbers represents a different acquisition policy.

poses of comparison. The use of Roman numerals indicates that the priority numbers used are those stipulated in the acquisition policy, as will be the case throughout this chapter. Under the General European Collection and the first column of priority numbers, we see that the emphasis of the library is on the history of each country, with the literature of France, Great Britain, and Spain falling into a category of secondary importance, philosophy of third importance, and science last. This means, theoretically, that if enough funds were available for only the first two priorities, history and literature would receive them. In the second budgetary priority list we see a totally different pattern, for here the priorities indicate that the main emphasis is on a single nation and not on a particular aspect such as history or science. Thus the second column of priority numbers reveals that all the first priority funding is to be spent on France, with Spain in second place and Great Britain in third. If there were funds available for only the first two priority ranks, then Great Britain would be omitted completely. In the third column of priority numbers (again a separate set of acquisition policy numbers) we see a special relationship between France and Great Britain in the fields of history and literature, with Spain falling into second place in these two categories, philosophy ranking third for all three countries, and science fourth.

Restricted or endowed funds mean automatic funding for each of the three special collections, though establishing the sub-priorities within each would probably be done by the curator unless, of course, the acquisition policy states this. In Figure 5 of the A Foundation for Danish Literature we see in the first column that the period of 1649–1900 receives first consideration, 1400–1648 receives second, and medieval literature receives the lowest priority. In the second column (established by an alternate acquisition policy) for this same subject, we see 1400–1648 receiving first priority, the medieval period again second, and the most recent period the lowest priority. In the third separate budget, under Danish Literature, the policy reflects another totally different approach, requiring equal expenditure and development of each of the three chronological periods.

In the case of the B Foundation for American Indians, the subcategories are divided not by time but by geography. In the first column, North American Indians receive top priority, Central American Indians second, and South American Indians third.

By establishing an internal priority system for each subject, one must not assume automatically that the same list of internal (i.e., interim) priorities should exist year after year, though the overall long-term priority numbers remain unchanged. Perhaps an unusually good collection is bought in one field, thereby requiring the transfer of funds from other fields. The following year, those funds can be reallocated to another sub-field within the overall priority, and an example of this will be seen shortly. For example, suppose an unusually strong Spanish philosophy collection can be purchased this year though this is not a main priority, then the following year one can shift the priority back to history or literature. Or in the event that a significant donation of books in one specific area is received, then funds that would have ordinarily gone to that field may be reallocated to another. In short, the acquisition policy must allow common sense to prevail, by allowing some elasticity, for after all the unusual collection being purchased in Spanish philosophy still falls within the bona fide collecting field of Spain as a stated priority. What will emerge, however, will be two sets of priority numbers for each budget, one the projected number of each sub-unit as dictated by the acquisition policy, and then later, when it actually comes to spending that budget, one reflecting any position of change, but keeping in mind all the while that *the acquisition policy priority number given to any sub-unit for a five-year period is the ultimate determining factor for the curator.* That final priority number is the recognized, authorized, ultimate goal.

But how would these priorities be applied in drawing up the budgetary request for the forthcoming fiscal year? The priority numbers would tentatively be replaced by the amounts of money, though what percentage of the total available in each category going to each priority would depend upon how the curator chose to allocate the funds, or if collecting "levels" have been previously established according to subject matter, they would dictate the level of expenditure. For example, if $100,000 were available, the curator could allocate $40,000 to the first priority, $25,000 to the second, $20,000 to the third, and $15,000 to the fourth (see Figure 6), or assign an equal amount to each unit or, for that matter, apply whatever he or she wished.

Let us say that $100,000 would have to be divided among the three categories of the General European Collection—France, Great Britain, and Spain—and then assigned by sub-category. Although it is possible to assign the entire sum to just one country, such as France, as seen in the second priority number column of Figure 5, it is much more likely that the amount would be divided evenly among the three, thus allowing approximately $33,333 per category. If, as in the first priority num-

### FIGURE 6   Assigning the Budget

I.  General European Collection.

    A.  France
        History                          $ 40,000
        Literature                         25,000
        Philosophy                         20,000
        Science                            15,000

    B.  Great Britain
        History                                 0
        Literature                              0
        Philosophy                              0
        Science                                 0

    C.  Spain
        History                                 0
        Literature                              0
        Philosophy                              0
        Science                                 0

ber column of Figure 5, the priorities went simply in consecutive order, the curator could divide each lump sum into four separate sums for each of the four sub-units. Naturally, the curator could decide equally to distribute the budget in the following manner allowing France $50,000, Spain $30,000, and Great Britain the remaining $20,000. In the event that the $100,000 would be divided into $33,333 for each of the three categories, such a budget could conceivably look like the one in Figure 7.

There is no end to the variants employable in allocating funds, but one thing is always true: the curator must know his or her collections very well and be able to establish priorities among the different collections and then within each collection. He or she must know what the *ultimate goals* are and where the decisions are to be made. This process may also serve as a sifting process and enable the curator to recognize areas that no longer fit into the long-term plan, as the Newberry Library discovered when it finally decided to sell off its Russian and Eastern European holdings. Curators may object that this is a long, trying process, but the system itself is basically simple, and it is, in any event, in the best interests of the collection. This process must be done formally so that the curator can see the results that emerge when the

FIGURE 7   Budget Distribution

I. General European Collection.

A. France
| | | |
|---|---|---|
| History | $ 12,000 | |
| Literature | 9,000 | |
| Philosophy | 7,000 | |
| Science | 5,334 | |
| | | $ 33,334 |

B. Great Britain
| | | |
|---|---|---|
| History | 15,000 | |
| Literature | 12,000 | |
| Philosophy | 6,333 | |
| Science | 0 | |
| | | 33,333 |

C. Spain
| | | |
|---|---|---|
| History | 8,334 | |
| Literature | 8,333 | |
| Philosophy | 8,333 | |
| Science | 8,333 | |
| | | 33,333 |
| | | $100,000 |

priority variants are laid out over several years. Collecting books should not be a guessing game, a hit-or-miss proposition. Control of the budget by using priorities can only strengthen a collection; it does not harm it.

It may appear that priorities fluctuate from year to year, yet in fact such fluctuations ultimately, over every five-year period, meet the priorities of that policy (see Figures 9 and 10). But in essence we are really talking about two five-year periods: the past five years—in order to assess what has or has not been achieved—and the next five years. Although most university libraries do this for the general library budget—as does Princeton, for instance—few special collections do this, though the process is as critical to their development as it is to the general library budget. Thus we are constantly looking at a block of ten years, the final half of which establishes clearly what has yet to be achieved in those remaining five years in order to maintain the priorities of the acquisition policy. Figure 8 provides an idealized pro-

## FIGURE 8   Ten-Year Expenditure

### A. Five-Year Actual Expenditure

|  |  | 1980-81 Actual | 1981-82 Actual | 1982-83 Actual | 1983-84 Actual | 1984-85 Budget | 1985-86 Requested |
|---|---|---|---|---|---|---|---|
| I. PERSONNEL |  |  |  |  |  |  |  |
| II. OPERATING EXPENSES |  |  |  |  |  |  |  |
| III. ACQUISITIONS |  |  |  |  |  |  |  |
| A. General |  |  |  |  |  |  |  |
| 1. France | | 16,000 | 20,000 | 24,000 | 29,000 | 33,334 | 36,334--Base + inflat.9% |
| 2. Great Brit. | | 16,000 | 20,000 | 24,000 | 29,000 | 33,334 | 36,334--Base + 9% |
| 3. Spain | | 16,000 | 20,000 | 24,000 | 29,000 | 33,334 | 36,334--Base + 9% |
| B. Endowed |  |  |  |  |  |  |  |
| 1. Danish Lit. | | 30,500 | 35,500 | 40,500 | 45,500 | 50,000 | 54,500--Base + inflat.9% |
| 2. Amer. Ind. | | 30,500 | 35,500 | 40,500 | 45,500 | 50,000 | 54,500--Base + inflat.9% |
| 3. Flor. Ren. | | 30,500 | 35,500 | 40,500 | 45,500 | 50,000 | 54,500--Base + inflat.9% |

### B. Projected Five-Year Expenditure

|  | 1986-87 Request | 1987-88 Project | 1988-89 Project | 1989-90 Project | 1990-91 Projected |
|---|---|---|---|---|---|
| I. PERSONNEL |  |  |  |  |  |
| II. OPERATING EXPENSES |  |  |  |  |  |
| III. ACQUISITIONS |  |  |  |  |  |
| A. General |  |  |  |  |  |
| 1. France | 36,334 | 39,604 | 43,163 | 47,054 | 51,289 |
| 2. Great Brit. | 36,333 | 39,603 | 43,162 | 47,053 | 51,288 |
| 3. Spain | 36,333 | 39,603 | 43,162 | 47,053 | 51,288 |
| B. Endowed |  |  |  |  |  |
| 1. Danish Lit. | 54,500 | 59,405 | 64,751 | 70,579 | 76,931 |
| 2. Amer. Ind. | 54,500 | 59,405 | 64,751 | 70,579 | 76,931 |
| 3. Flor. Ren. | 54,500 | 59,405 | 64,751 | 70,579 | 76,931 |

gression of such a system, without, however, revealing the multifarious internal annual shifts and changes.

In Figure 9, a five-year pattern illustrates some of the vicissitudes affecting year-to-year budgeting. It should be noted that there are two kinds of priority numbers used again here, as earlier in this chapter, the Roman numeral continuing to represent the acquisition policy objectives. All is subject to the unforeseen forces of the future and funding

## FIGURE 9   The Five-Year Budget by Priority Number

| | APPN 1981-82 | AN | APPN 1982-83 | AN | APPN 1983-84 | AN | APPN 1984-85 | AN | APPN 1985-86 | AN | Acq. Pol P.N. Five Yr. Result. |
|---|---|---|---|---|---|---|---|---|---|---|---|
| **I. General European Collection** | | | | | | | | | | | |
| **A. France** | | | | | | | | | | | |
| 1. History | I | 1 | I | 1 | I | 3 | I | 3 | I | 1 | I |
| 2. Literature | II | 2 | II | 0 | II | 1 | II | 1 | II | 2 | II |
| 3. Philosophy | III | 3 | III | 2 | III | 2 | III | 4 | III | 4 | III |
| 4. Science | IV | 4 | IV | 0 | IV | 4 | IV | 2 | IV | 3 | IV |
| **B. Great Britain** | | | | | | | | | | | |
| 1. History | I | 1 | I | 3 | I | 1 | I | 2 | I | 1 | I |
| 2. Literature | II | 2 | II | 1 | II | 2 | II | 1 | II | 4 | II |
| 3. Philosophy | III | 3 | III | 2 | III | 4 | III | 3 | III | 3 | III |
| 4. Science | IV | 4 | IV | 4 | IV | 3 | IV | 0 | IV | 2 | IV |
| **C. Spain** | | | | | | | | | | | |
| 1. History | I | 1 | I | 1 | I | 2 | I | 3 | I | 1 | I |
| 2. Literature | II | 2 | II | 3 | II | 1 | II | 2 | II | 2 | II |
| 3. Philosophy | III | 3 | III | 2 | III | 3 | III | 1 | III | 0 | III |
| 4. Science | IV | 4 | IV | 4 | IV | 4 | IV | 4 | IV | 4 | IV |
| **II. Special Endowed Collection** | | | | | | | | | | | |
| **A. The A Foundation, Danish Literature** | | | | | | | | | | | |
| 1. Medieval | III | 3 | III | 2 | III | 0 | III | 2 | III | 2 | III |
| 2. 1400-1648 | I | 1 | I | 1 | I | 1 | I | 1 | I | 1 | I |
| 3. 1649-1900 | II | 2 | II | 3 | II | 1 | II | 3 | II | 1 | II |
| **B. The B Foundation, American Indians** | | | | | | | | | | | |
| 1. No. Amer. | III | 3 | III | 0 | III | 2 | III | 2 | III | 3 | III |
| 2. Cent. Amer. | II | 2 | II | 0 | II | 1 | II | 3 | II | 2 | II |
| 3. So. Amer. | I | 1 | I | 1 | I | 0 | I | 1 | I | 1 | I |
| **C. The C Foundation, Florentine Renaissance** | | | | | | | | | | | |
| 1. Art | I | 1 | I | 1 | I | 1 | I | 3 | I | 3 | I |
| 2. Literature | II | 2 | II | 2 | II | 0 | II | 1 | II | 2 | II |
| 3. Medicine | III | 0 | III | 0 | III | 0 | III | 2 | III | 1 | III |

APPN = Acquisition Policy Priority Number projected for that year.
AN   = The actual priority number given that year.
The final column, Acq. Pol. P.N., shows exactly what the average Priority Number came to over a period of five years.

fluctuations could require continued replanning, just as a sailor must sometimes hastily chart a new course when blown off the old one. In Figure 10 we can see both sets of priority numbers (the acquisition policy priority numbers in the far right-hand column) as well as an actual budget. The "Five-Year Total" establishes how much was spent in the five-year span for each period, and this may be compared then with the acquisition policy priority number beside it in the final column.

APN  = Actual, annual priority number
APPN = Acquisition policy priority number

## FIGURE 10   The Five-Year Budget

| | 1981-82 | APN | 1982-83 | APN | 1983-84 | APN | 1984-85 | APN | 1985-86 | APN | 5 YR. TOTAL | A.P. P.N. |
|---|---|---|---|---|---|---|---|---|---|---|---|---|
| **I. General European Collection** | | | | | | | | | | | | |
| **A. France** | | | | | | | | | | | | |
| 1. History | 12,000 | 1 | 25,000 | 1 | 5,000 | 3 | 6,000 | 3 | 12,000 | 1 | 60,000 | I |
| 2. Literature | 9,000 | 2 | 0 | 0 | 15,000 | 1 | 12,000 | 1 | 9,000 | 2 | 45,000 | II |
| 3. Philosophy | 7,000 | 3 | 8,334 | 2 | 9,000 | 2 | 5,332 | 4 | 5,334 | 4 | 35,000 | III |
| 4. Science | 5,334 | 4 | 0 | 0 | 4,332 | 4 | 10,000 | 2 | 7,000 | 3 | 26,662 | IV |
| **B. Great Britain** | | | | | | | | | | | | |
| 1. History | 12,000 | 1 | 7,000 | 3 | 19,000 | 1 | 12,400 | 2 | 12,000 | 1 | 60,000 | I |
| 2. Literature | 9,000 | 2 | 12,000 | 1 | 6,000 | 2 | 15,000 | 1 | 3,000 | 4 | 45,000 | II |
| 3. Philosophy | 7,000 | 3 | 9,000 | 2 | 5,000 | 4 | 6,334 | 3 | 7,666 | 3 | 35,000 | III |
| 4. Science | 5,333 | 4 | 5,333 | 4 | 5,333 | 3 | 0 | 0 | 9,665 | 2 | 26,662 | IV |
| **C. Spain** | | | | | | | | | | | | |
| 1. History | 12,000 | 1 | 12,000 | 1 | 9,000 | 2 | 7,000 | 3 | 20,000 | 1 | 60,000 | I |
| 2. Literature | 9,000 | 2 | 7,000 | 3 | 12,000 | 1 | 9,000 | 2 | 8,000 | 2 | 45,000 | II |
| 3. Philosophy | 7,000 | 3 | 9,000 | 2 | 7,000 | 3 | 12,000 | 1 | 0 | 0 | 35,000 | III |
| 4. Science | 5,333 | 4 | 5,333 | 4 | 5,333 | 4 | 5,333 | 4 | 5,333 | 4 | 26,662 | IV |
| **II. Special, Endowed Collections** | | | | | | | | | | | | |
| **A. The A Foundation, Danish Literature** | | | | | | | | | | | | |
| 1. Medieval | 10,000 | 3 | 15,000 | 2 | 0 | 0 | 15,000 | 2 | 10,000 | 2 | 50,000 | III |
| 2. 1400-1648 | 25,000 | 1 | 25,000 | 1 | 25,000 | 1 | 30,000 | 1 | 20,000 | 1 | 125,000 | II |
| 3. 1649-1900 | 15,000 | 2 | 10,000 | 3 | 25,000 | 1 | 5,000 | 3 | 20,000 | 1 | 75,000 | II |
| **B. The B Foundation, American Indians** | | | | | | | | | | | | |
| 1. No. Amer. | 10,000 | 3 | 0 | 0 | 15,000 | 2 | 15,000 | 2 | 10,000 | 3 | 50,000 | III |
| 2. Cent. Amer. | 15,000 | 2 | 0 | 0 | 35,000 | 1 | 10,000 | 3 | 15,000 | 2 | 75,000 | II |
| 3. So. Amer. | 25,000 | 1 | 50,000 | 1 | 0 | 0 | 25,000 | 1 | 25,000 | 1 | 125,000 | I |
| **C. The C Foundation, Florentine Renaissance** | | | | | | | | | | | | |
| 1. Art | 25,000 | 1 | 35,000 | 1 | 50,000 | 1 | 5,000 | 3 | 10,000 | 3 | 125,000 | I |
| 2. Literature | 15,000 | 2 | 15,000 | 2 | 0 | 0 | 30,000 | 1 | 15,000 | 2 | 75,000 | II |
| 3. Medicine | 10,000 | 3 | 0 | 0 | 0 | 0 | 15,000 | 2 | 25,000 | 1 | 50,000 | III |

In Figure 10 (the Five-Year Budget) I have deliberately tried to cause as much havoc as possible in the fluctuation and allocation of funds channeled to each sub-priority. Despite these annual changes, the curator must always keep an eye on the acquisition policy priority number in the right-hand column and juggle the budget so that *by the end of that five-year period the funds spent in each area match the priority number of the last column.* In reality the budget usually will not be subject to such great variations, but the simple concept of budget priorities does clearly establish that, regardless of the varied changes over a period of years, approximately the same amount will be spent on each priority in the long run, just as if an equal amount had been spent annually.

Hence the great virtues of this system are twofold: *the curator is never allowed to lose sight of priorities and knows well in advance where and how to shift funds to match expected expenditure by priority for each five-year period,* thereby emerging at the end of that period with more or less precisely the development anticipated, dictated, and charted by the acquisition policy. The second virtue of this system is its *flexibility.* It allows for even the most drastic of fluctuations on an annual basis, without affecting the anticipated cumulative result.

It is useful to observe some of the more singular transactions in Figure 10. In the first column, for 1981–1982, all budgets for all subjects were distributed in textbook fashion, according to their acquisition policy priority number, and all received the correct allocations. Under ordinary circumstances most budgets would be fairly similar to this, year after year, but in this example things have changed for the worse. In the 1982–83 column we can see that in the case of France something extraordinary has happened. The usual $12,000 budget for History has been more than doubled to reach a figure of $25,000, and the budget for Philosophy is slightly above normal, $8,334, as opposed to $7,000, while the usual $9,000 budget for Literature and $5,334 for Science have disappeared completely. When one sub-unit such as Literature receives less than usual, that amount must be made up over the remaining part of the five-year period and, in the case of Literature, we see that the additional $9,000 is added above the normal budgets in 1983–84 and 1984–85, so that by 1985–86 it is back to normal, or $9,000. When one looks at the overall budget for French Literature for the entire five-year period, one sees that the acquisition policy priority number allotted to this field, II, was adhered to and that therefore that sub-unit was increased precisely as anticipated five years earlier.

When in the case of History the budget is more than doubled in 1982–83, that means that the following budgets are greatly reduced until the normal budget can be reached, thereby enabling the five-year total expenditure to reach the projected amount, in this case, $60,000, adhering to the acquisition policy priority number, I, as anticipated. The rationale for such an unusual one-time expenditure in the field of History could be simply the need to purchase a unique private collection in this field, filling a major gap in the holdings. At the same time, the number-two priority for that year is shifted to Philosophy, which receives what remains of the budget (perhaps some special works in that field had long been needed), whereas in the field of Literature there are no immediately pressing needs. Science, too, goes without funding that year. Throughout this process, the flexibility needed was indeed employed. Had the curator kept to a rigid priority expenditure scheme year by year, it will be argued that the sub-units of History, or Literature, for instance, would have spent the same amounts over the five-year-period, which is true. On the other hand, without that flexibility, the library would frequently be forced to forego acquiring important, unique, and expensive collections that might suddenly become available, though the funds might have been available within the total annual budget. (One alternative for this would be for the curator to develop a special independent contingency allocations fund to meet such needs.) But to return to the three collection areas of France, Great Britain, and Spain when allotted an equal $33,333 annually, established over a five-year period, the figures in the right-hand column of Figure 10—of $60,000, $45,000, $35,000, and $26,662 per year—would be reached within each of those national categories.

But there is another factor which could very easily cause those three categories in the general collection to end up with different totals at the end of a five-year period if, for example, donations in the form of books were added. Let us say that in a given fiscal year French History was given a donation of books worth $20,000. How would the curator then treat the budget for the other sub-units of France? One option is simply to allocate funds by making priority 2 now priority 1, making priority 3 now 2, and moving 4 up to 3, but increasing the amounts to cover each sub-unit. Literature might receive $14,500, Philosophy, $11,500, and Science $7,334. Thus the entire annual budget of $33,333 would be spent as usual, though the total increase in value of acquisitions for that year would rise by $53,333, thanks to the donation of books. But in fact there is no hard and fast rule for the curator to follow in this case; the key is to maintain more or less proportional development of each each sub-unit when it comes time to assess the results of five years' acquisitions.

There are other types of priority programs, of course, ones which allow for no flexibility, and Stueart and Eastlick provide an example in the case of a small town library which lists its priorities one through nine, but having only $107,200 to commit immediately for the year, can only fully and effectively fund the first four priorities, thereby rendering the remaining five programs inoperative for the moment.[14] The curator would have a choice of adopting this sort of rigid annual allocation, and of course it would require much less thought and work on the part of the curator, but would it really be in the best interests of the collection development policy? A small town library does not have the same goals and objectives as a research library's special collection—large or small—and the annual programs rarely have any unusual needs, such as the acquisition of a private collection of choice rare materials just put on the market.

A flexible system of intermediate priorities, enforced and shaped by the general acquisition policy priority numbers, allows the greatest opportunity for the developing of a special collection of unusual quality and distinction.

## References

1. This example is based on a form used by Stueart and Eastlick, although the figures are mine. Robert D. Stueart and John T. Eastlick, *Library Management* (Littleton, Colo.: Libraries Unlimited, 1971), p. 162. See also Peter Spyers-Duran, *Prediction of Resource Needs: A Model Budget Formula for Upper Division University Libraries.* This doctoral thesis for Nova University was later published by Xerox Univerity Microfilms, Ann Arbor, Mich., 1975, pp. 15 ff.
2. *Preparation and Presentation of the Library Budget.* SPEC Kit 32, April 1977, p. 1. The Systems & Procedures Exchange Center, Association of Research Libraries, Office of Management Studies, Washington, D.C. See also B. Allen, "Administration of Grant Funds—The Project Approach," *Collection Management,* 5 (Fall-Winter 1983), 175–184; D.M. Goehner, "Allocating by Formula; The Rationale from an Institutional Perspective," *Collection Management,* 5 (Fall-Winter 1983), 161-173; G. M.

Shirk, "Allocation Formulas for Budgeting Library Materials: Science or Procedure?" *Collection Management,* 6 (Fall-Winter 1984), 37-47; and G. B. McCabe, *Austerity Management in Academic Libraries* (Metuchen, N.J.: Scarecrow Press, 1984.

3. Harry Williams, *Planning for Effective Resource Allocations in Universities* (Washington, D.C.: American Council in Education, 1966), p. 15.

4. James Farmer, *Why Planning, Programming, Budgeting Systems for Higher Education?* (Boulder, Colo.: Western Interstate Commission for Higher Education, 1970), p. 8.

5. Guy J. De Genaro, *A Planning-Programming-Budgeting System in Academic Libraries,* Ph.D. thesis, University of Florida, 1971, p. 146.

6. Spyers-Duran, p. 65.

7. Elise Hayton, "Zero Base Budgeting in a University Library," *Special Libraries,* 65 (Fall 1979), 371–82.

8. Rodney M. Hersberger, "Zero Base Budgeting: A Library Example," *Catholic Library World,* 51, No. 4 (Nov. 1979), 158–61.

9. Anne G. Sarndal, "Zero Base Budgeting," *Special Libraries,* 70, No. 2 (Dec. 1979), 527–32.

10. Stueart and Eastlick provide a similar form, p. 173. For a step-by-step study of the ZBB process, see C.C. Chen, *Zero-Base Budgeting in Library Management. A Manual for Librarians* (Phoenix: Oryx Press, 1980).

11. "Standards of College Libraries," *College and Research Libraries,* 20 (July 1959), 274–80.

12. Vernon W. Clapp and Robert T. Jordan, "Quantitative Criteria for Adequacy of Academic Library Collections," *College and Research Libraries,* 25 (Sept. 1965), 371–80.

13. Spyers-Duran, p. 65.

14. Stueart and Eastlick, p. 174.

# 3

# Classifying, Cataloging, and Automation

## CLASSIFYING AND CATALOGING

A considerable variety of systems is used in classifying and cataloging books and manuscripts in this country and abroad. Yale follows the Library of Congress classification system, the Vatican follows the Dewey decimal system, and the Bibliothèque Nationale and Archives Nationales adhere to various acquisition series, subdivided by subjects. The classification of manuscripts falls into a separate and unique category offering numerous different approaches. For example, the reports drawn up by Captain Marchand (during the famous Fashoda incident of 1898) for the Minister of Foreign Affairs are to be found in the French National Archives listed:

Section Outre-mer
*Série Missions*
Missions 42
Missions 43

while the French ministerial communications concerning Fashoda are classified under:

Section Outre-Mer
*Série Afrique:*
Afrique III 33

Meanwhile, the private papers of members of the mission are located in the Archives Nationales, under Fonds Privés (e.g., 99AP 3, for

Baratier; and 149 AP 3, for Mangin), while at the Bibliothèque Nationale it is the series acquisition numerical designation which is used, the name of the collection, or the manuscript number, as in the following examples:

> Nouv. Acq. Fr. 232, Fol. 4, Letter of Henri III to Cardinal de Lorraine, dated 18 Nov. 1572
> Coll. Touraine 10, Fol. 257, Letter of Henri III to the Comte du Lude [Nov., 1572]
> Ms. Fr. 3249, Fol. 44, Letter of Henri III to Maréchale de Damville, 11 Nov. 1572.

Records in London concerning the Foreign Office are issued through the Public Record Office under an alphanumeric designation for the country and the year, as seen in the following examples:

> FO 1 (Abyssinia), 1897-9
> FO 2 (Africa), 1893-9
> FO 27 (France), 1894-9
> FO 146 (France: Embassy Archives), 1898-9

Other libraries and archives devise still different means of classifying manuscripts. For instance, the papers of Lord Salisbury are housed in the Archives of Christ Church College, Oxford, according to the subject, geographical point of emanation, and year:

> A/111 Egypt and Fashoda
> A/116 (Diplomatic correspondence from France to England)
> A/119 (Salisbury to France)

The Sudan Archive, at the University of Durham, England, gives a number to each subject, followed by the carton number:

> 102/1 Wingate diary
> 233/5 Wingate correspondence with wife
> 441/3 Diaries of Slatin Pasha

Specially devised classification designations are not limited to foreign countries. The system created for the printed works of the Hunt Institute for Botanical Documentation (Figure 1), is further refined by including a Cutter number for its author and the year published (if it is not the first edition):

FIGURE 1   The Hunt Classification Schedule

| | |
|---|---|
| A-AE | Agriculture |
| B-BMI | General science, excluding agriculture, botany, and horticulture. |
| C-CG | Herbals |
| D-DT100 | Botany |
| E-EP | Horticulture |
| F-FH | Landscape Architecture |
| G-GK | Fine Arts |
| K | History and Geography |
| L-LC | Biology |
| M-MC | Travels |
| N-NR | Bibliography |
| P | Periodicals |
| Pl | Bibliography of Periodicals |

The variations in attempts to decide what a descriptive catalog should include, and how it should be done, are equally numerous, and sometimes so different as to give rise to heated discussions by incensed catalogers and librarians who refuse to accept the validity of more than one system. Naturally, there is no single valid descriptive cataloging system, as both Bowers and McKerrow have acknowledged.[1] Fredson Bowers' explanation of how the methods of descriptive bibliography have evolved to achieve their triple purpose is nearly complete.[2]

(1) to furnish a detailed, analytical record of the physical characteristics of a book which would simultaneously serve as a trustworthy source of identification and as a medium to bring an absent book before a reader's eyes; (2) to provide an analytical investigation and an ordered arrangement of these physical facts which would serve as the prerequisite for textual criticism of the book described; (3) to approach both literary and printing or publishing history through the investigation and recording of appropriate details in a related series of books.

But despite acknowledged differences, the American Library Association's *Anglo-American Cataloguing Rules 2* (AACR2) publishes one agreed-upon system which is increasingly used and which tallies with the Library of Congress and the MARC (machine-readable cataloging) System. This has in turn resulted in the publication of the *Bibliographic Description of Rare Books* by the Library of Congress, adhering to the rules of AACR2 and the International Standard Bibliographical Description (Antiquarian), or ISBD (A). The following are two examples of cataloging as "suggested" by the *Bibliographic Description of Rare Books:*[3] For the purist, however, the catalog descriptions in Figure 2 are less than adequate. The titles are shortened, colophons are not quoted, there are no signatures, and there is no reference to the watermark, the type used, the paper, or even the binding.

The Hunt Institute used to provide an exemplary catalog of the way many felt that very rare books should be cataloged, as seen in Allan Stevenson's famous second volume published for the Hunt.[4] Over the past several years, however, even the Hunt has simplified its catalog descriptions so that it is now closer to the examples seen in Figure 2 than the example of Stevenson's work seen in Figure 3 (on pages 48–49). Though the number of plates is still listed, collations, colophons, watermarks, types of binding, etc., are now omitted, as are references to other bibliographical citations and references.

One of the major changes occurring in catalog descriptions everywhere is the general shortening of the average catalog information, partly in response to adaptation to automation and storage requirements allowed in databases—examples of these printouts will be seen later—but also because librarians frequently can no longer check and record the collation, the misprinted paginations, the missing tip-ins, etc., because their staffs have been so greatly reduced that time and demand no longer permit this work to be done, and thus they gladly endorse the views of the *AACR2.* And, some ask, does it really matter if the first and third editions are so very different, or whether the cover is "rubbed," or whether it is original or all leather, or quarter-calf, or of vellum or of crushed morocco, or that the book is printed by a master craftsman? Have we arrived at a point when the past no longer seems to count for much? One is not so terribly short of the mark when comparing the value and "relevance" of rare works in our society to that of any other "dinosaur."

## CLASSIFICATION AND ORGANIZATION TILL THE 19TH CENTURY

Let's look briefly at how we have attempted to classify and organize materials over the centuries. In the fifth century B.C. it does

## FIGURE 2  Illustrations of Antiquarian Cataloging According to AACR2

1.       The works of the late Right Honorable Joseph
         Addison, Esq; : with a complete index.  -- Birmingham
         :  Printed by John Baskerville, for J. and R. Tonson
         ... London, 1761.

            4 v. : ill., port. ; 30 cm. (4to)

            Vol. 1: xxv, [3], 537 [5], 415-525 (i.e. 415-
         537), [5] p., [4] leaves of plates; v. 2: [8], 538,
         [14] p.; v. 3: 579, [13] p.; 4: 555, [13] p. Last
         leaves of v. 2 and 4 blank.  Page 537 of last
         numbered sections of v. 1 misnumered 525.
            References:  Gaskell, P. J. Baskerville 17.
            Contents:  v. 1. Preface.  Poems on several occasions.
         Rosamond. An essay on Virgil's Georgics. Cato. The
         drummer, or, The haunted house.  Poemata.  Dialogues
         upon the usefulness of ancient medals -- v. 2.
         Remarks on several parts of Italy, &c. The Tatler.
         The Spectator, no. 1-89 -- v. 3.  The Spectator,
         no. 90-505 -- v. 4.  The Spectator, no. 507-600.
         The guardian.  The Lover. The present states of
         the war, and the necessity of an augmentation,
         considered.  The Whig-examiner, the Free-holder.
         Of the Christian religion.
            LC copy:  In v. 1 leaves Zzzz2-3 incorrectly
         bound before Zzz1.  Vol. 2 lacks the blank at the
         end.

2.       Priuilegia clerico[rum] [et] queda[m] alia vtilia
         his continentur ... -- [Augsburg] : Impressa. . .
         Auguste per Iohanne[m] Froschauer, 1498.

            [16] leaves (the last blank) ; 19 cm. (4to)

            Imprint from colophon.
            References:  (from t.p.) Constitutio Friderici
         Imperatoris -- Constitutio Karoli Quarti Imperatoris
         que nominatur Karolina -- Constitutio Sigismundi
         Imperatoris que nominatur Sigismundina continentes in
         se priuilegia [et] immunitates clericorum -- Bonifacij
         Pape constitutio [per] qua[m] co[n]firmat supradicta
         priuilegia, a tribus Imperatoribus clericis co[n] cessa
         -- Item Honorius Papa constitutione[m] Friderici
         Imperatoris approbauit [et] confirmauit -- Iohannes
         Papa xxiij eadem priuilegia co[n]firmauit -- Consiliu[m]
         Lateranense [et] Basiliense eadem priuilegia clericoru[m]
         [et] constituiones Imperatoru[m] approbaru[n]t [et]
         confirmarunt -- Vtrum clerici teneantur de fundibus suis,
         domibus, agris [et] similibus tributa [et] exactiones dare,
         et an tenean [tur] ad onera personalia.

not seem that written materials were organized with any more care and respect than bills of lading for ships entering and leaving the Piraeus. Moreover, many forms of pre-Greek cataloging and inventory schemes that originated in the Middle East have probably escaped us permanently, hidden beneath the rubble of centuries and the tank tracks and bomb and rocket craters of our own century.

In the West we go back to the arrangement of elementary knowledge by Francis Bacon, the First Baron of Verulam (modern St. Albans), and later Viscount.[5] This is fairly recent, of course, but at least some sort of methodology was applied, even if we are talking about the sixteenth and seventeenth centuries. To Bacon in the early seventeenth century, knowledge fell into three general categories: history, philosophy, and poetry. History according to him was composed of four divisions—natural, civil, ecclesiastical, and literary; philosophy included theology and the thoughts and values of individuals. Poetry (as distinguished from "literature") concerned values and the imagination. All this Bacon duly recorded in an encyclopedia of all knowledge, his *Instauratio Magna.* In 1620, not long before his death, he wrote his celebrated *Novum Organum,* the key to his new systematic analysis of knowledge, intended, he said, to replace the deductive logic of Aristotle with inductive interpretation. Bacon no doubt would have been pleased to see his system taken so seriously so many years later, for elements of it were adopted by Thomas Jefferson when planning the University of Virginia. Many elements were also accepted by Benjamin Franklin when he created the Library Company of Philadelphia, following the American Revolution, three years before Jefferson's *Catalogue of the Library of the United States* was placed in the Library of Congress, and later another variant appeared in 1812 in the *Catalogue of the Library of Congress.* Meanwhile, in France, still following Bacon's system, Jean LeRond d' Alembert published the *Encyclopédie ou Dictionnaire Raisonné des Sciences des Métiers.* This was followed by adaptations to the age of utilitarianism by French libraries when Jacques Charles Brunet[6] created utilitarian classification schemes which were applied in Richelieu's former palace, the Bibliothèque Nationale. In this country William Torrey Harris was developing his own Hegelian system, which a young American undergraduate was soon to absorb and develop further, with remarkable ramifications.

## MODERN CLASSIFICATION AND ORGANIZATION

The first significant "modern statement of principles"[7] was applied by Panizzi's *British Museum Rules for the Compiling of the Catalogues* nearly twenty years before the outbreak of the American Civil War. In 1876, when Melvil Dewey devised his Dewey decimal classification, much of which he based on William Harris's earlier work, but adding his own famous touch, the decimal notation, the library world was going through a silent revolution, though it may not have realized it at once. Obviously, classifications and systems can be approached with many viewpoints. Charles Cutter was more interested in establishing a better means of arranging books than in creating an entirely new classification scheme, but there were others. James Duff Brown developed subject classifications (based on categorical and biographical tables), and Henry Bliss's system suggested subjects according to "natural order" which included historical general works first, then works in general subjects treated specifically, then works on special subjects treated generally, and finally, works on specific subjects treated specifically.

The nineteenth and twentieth centuries have been fertile in awareness of and in ideas concerning the collation of library materials, much of it stimulated by advances in the sciences. Cutter's *Rules for a Printed Dictionary Catalogue* and *Expansive Classification* were brought out by 1904. Meanwhile, the Library of Congress's *Rules on Printed Cards* had appeared in 1903, though it was not until 1949 that the LC's *Rules for Descriptive Cataloguing* was published. The American Library Association had first come out with its own cataloging rules as early as 1908, followed in 1967 by the *Anglo-American Cataloging Rules* and, of course, by the *AACR2* now in use. The International Standard Bibliographic Description (ISBD) was introduced in the United States in 1974 in an effort to provide uniform elements of information about each publication, in agreement with numerous foreign countries, thereby creating an International Standard Book (or Serial) Number with an added category (A) for antiquarian works.

## DIFFERENT DESCRIPTIVE APPROACHES

The Library of Congress has published a separate volume for the cataloging of rare books, entitled *Bibliographic Description of Rare*

*Books, Rules Formulated Under the AACR2 and ISBD(A) for the Descriptive Cataloguing of Rare Books and Other Special Printed Materials.* This work keeps rigidly to specific rules and to the the the MARC format, which some rare book curators feel very uneasy with, as Roderick Cave attests in his excellent work, *Rare Book Librarianship.*[8] "The relative inhospitability of cataloging codes like AACR2 and MARC format for the special needs of rare book cataloging have been a cause of concern to the Independent Research Libraries Association and others who fear that modern methods of storing and disseminating catalog information will not unless modified be in the interests of users or custodians of rare book collections." Cave finds particular fault with the usual library techniques used for cataloging letters and other manuscript materials, which instead require special considerations.[9]

Underlining the unique qualities of each special collection, Cave emphasizes the importance of the techniques employed to catalog and describe them and that they be capable of being molded to fit the collection, hence the inadequacy of blindly applying one rigid code. He provides an excellent example when referring to the Hunt Institute's singular collection of rare works on botany, the catalog of which was so carefully treated by Allan Stevenson in his "Bibiliographical Method for the Description of Botanical Books."[10] "Undeservedly neglected," he writes, "this section explains the function and importance of the various elements in a way which can be appreciated by the botanical reader as well as by the bibliographer." A catalog description is written for at least two different kinds of readers: for the librarian, but also for the scholar. Figure 3 shows a fairly typical example of Stevenson's work, which is complete down to the description of the paper, type, and bindings and also includes notes on the significance of this work and its later influence upon Linnaeus.[11] The Stevenson catalog is both formal and complete for both the librarian and the scholar and naturally follows the methods of Greg and Bowers, expanding on Bowers's third category mentioned earlier in this chapter.

These examples illustrate how important it is for the catalog description to include ample notes on the significance of both the edition and subject work at hand. Notes can explain more fully the unique contents of works, frequently tucked away in an obscure appendix, and which, if not mentioned in the note, might very well be missed by the scholar, who may have limited time and who in some cases must rely heavily on the information provided by the card or printed catalog,

FIGURE 3    Vaillant's *Discours Sur La Structure des Fleurs,*
in *The Hunt Botanical Catalogue*

446   VAILLANT, Sébastien (1669-1722), French botanist, director of the Jardin du Roi.

*Discours sur la structure des fleurs. Sermo de structura florum.* Leyden 1718. *Kl. post 4°.*

DISCOURS I SUR LA STRUCTURE DES I FLEURS, I LEURS DIF-FERENCES ET L'USAGE I DE LEURS PARTIES; I Prononcé a l'Ouverture du Jardin Royal de Paris, I le X^e. Jour du mois de Juin 1717. I ET I L'ETABLISSEMENT I *de trois nouveaux genres de* I PLANTES, I L'ARALIASTRUM, I LA SHERARDIA, I LA BOERHAAVIA. I *Avec la Defcription de deux nouvelles* PLANTES I *rapportées au dernier genre,* I Par I SEBASTIEN VAILLANT, I *Demonftrateur des Plantes du Jardin Royal à Paris.* I [Engraved vignette: in background a city square, in foreground within a frame a man sawing through a block which bears the motto 'Tempore I & I INDUSTRIA.'; 2.2 × 4.6".] I *A LEIDE,* I Chez PIERRE VANDER A a, I *Marchand Libraire, Imprimeur de l'Université & de la Ville.* I —— I MDCCXVIII.

SERMO I DE I STRUCTURA I FLORUM, I HORUM DIFFERENTIA, USUQUE PAR- I TIUM EOS CONSTITUENTIUM, Habitus in ipfis aufpiciis Demonftrationis publicae Stir- I pium in Horto Regio Parifino, X°.-Junii 1717. I ET I CONSTITUTIO I *Trium novorum generum* I *PLAN-TARUM,* I *ARALIASTRI,* I *SHERARDIAE,* I *BOERHAAVIAE.* I *Cum descriptione duarum* PLANTARUM *novarum* I *generi postremo inscriptarum,* I Per I SEBASTIANUM VAILLANT, I *Demonstratorem Plantarum Horti Regii Parnftenfis.* I [Engraving identical with that on French title opposite] I *LUGDUNI BATAVORUM,* I *Apud* PETRUM VANDER A a, I *Bibliopolam,* Academiœque ut & Urbis Typographum Ordinarium. I —— I MDCCXVIII.

COLLATION: 4° : π² A-G⁴; [iv] I-55 [I]. πI^V: French title, r □. π2: Latin title, v □. AI: Publisher's preface. AI^V : French text in italic, headed 'DISCOURS I *Sur la Structure des Fleurs,* . . . ', continued on versos. A2 : Latin text in roman, headed 'SERMO I *Super fabricâ Florum,* . . . ', continued on rectos. E_4^V : '*ETABLISSEMENT* I *d'un nouveau genre de Plante nommé* I ARALIASTRUM, I . . . ', continued on versos. FI: 'CONSTITUTIO I *Novi Plantarum generis, quod nominatur* I ARALIAS-TRUM, I . . . ', continued on rectos. G4^V: errata. RTs: 'DISCOURS SUR LA I STRUCTURE DES FLEURS, &c.' 'DESCRIPTION DE I L'ARA-LIASTRUM.', 'DESCRIPTION DE DEUX I NOUVEAUX GENRES DE PLANTES.'

PAPER: *Kl. post or Kl. mediaan,* Dutch, unmarked. Leaf 8.9 × 7.2".

TYPE: *Augustijn* roman and italic 47: A3 = 36 lines. Preface: *tekst* roman 58.

BINDING: Tan paper boards; tan backstrip.

REFERENCES: Pritzel 9654, Haller; BM(NH), MH-A, MoSB, Kew, Lind. *Copies* (NUC+): MB (1717), NN (1717), PPAN (also 1717).

NOTES: Vaillant was a brilliant student of Tournefort's who became Director of the Jardin du Roi at Paris. The *Discours* was his first important work; and there were further editions or issues in 1727 and 1728. His great work, published after his death by Boerhaave, was *Botanicon Parisiense, ou Dénombrement . . . des plantes, qui se trouve aux environs de Paris* (1727) F°, with 33 plates by Claude Aubriet: Hunt 470. On Vaillant see Davy de Virville, pp. 39-40. Tournefort gave the name *Vaillantia* to a genus of the *Rubiaceae,* and Linnaeus accepted it (as *Valantia*).

Though Pritzel and the usual catalogues gave the date of the *Discours* as 1718, it is evident from NUC that some copies of the first edition are dated 1717. The 1718 copies must represent a second *issue.*

The *Discours sur la structure des fleurs* greatly influenced Linnaeus during his student days. He first knew of Vaillant's work through his teacher Rothman, but did not see the book until later. B. D. Jackson, biographer of Linnaeus notes:

> Herein the sexuality of plants was set forth as an indisputable fact. Linnaeus was warmly attracted by these new views and therefore he began to examine flowers for stamens and pistils, soon finding that they were not less different than the petals, and were the essential parts of the flower.

And on New Year's day 1730 he presented his benefactor Celsius with his first essay on the marriage of plants. (Benjamin D. Jackson, *Linnaeus* (1923), pp. 45-46.) In a letter to Haller Linnaeus acknowledged his debt to Vaillant: 'Chaque jour j'acquiers l'assurance que personne n'a été plus habile dans l'établissement des genres.'

Of the three new genera proposed by Vaillant in the *Discours,* Linnaeus treated *Sherardia* Vaill. as *Verbena* (now separated as *Phyla*), *Boerhaavia,* and classed *Araliastrum* as *Panax* (ginseng).

---

without having an opportunity to peruse each work. This is a very real factor, and hence the greater importance of a well prepared note. After all, it is easier for the reader to go through a seven-card catalog description than a thousand pages of text! Thus I believe that all content notes should include "the significance of this work," in at least a few lines. In many special collections departments today one frequently comes across younger librarians who are not always familiar with the major works in the collection, lacking linguistic, historical, and literary background, and in consequence have no idea what they are cataloging. This was brought home to me recently when going through the card catalog of a special collection and finding a famous Latin work listed under an obscure title, and in the wrong place, because the local cataloger could not read the Latin, was unfamiliar with the author, and therefore did not realize that the tome was simply the third volume of a world-famous philosophical treatise which came under a different title. Naturally, there was no reference to any of this in the note. If the cataloger had done a little more research, he or she would have found "The Significance of This Work" and would not have created so much inconvenience and frustration.

But lack of time, fewer trained bibliographical personnel, and lack of money have hurt rare book cataloging and special collections today. This is reflected in briefer catalog card descriptions, a problem which it appears each library must face individually. This problem is illustrated in the following section of this chapter.


## AUTOMATION

Rare book librarians have a special love of old books; each volume is a special treasure. Don Quixote fought windmills and the values of his age, and we—in what James Thurber no doubt would have referred to as a dog-cat relationship—are forced to accept what we sometimes feel to be the intrusion of computers, networks, and the centrifugal force carrying with it AACR2 and MARC format cards, known as "uniformity."

Rare book bibliographical information was first recorded in the computerized network systems such as OCLC and RLIN, in order to help the scholar or curator of rare books locate the nearest copy of the edition of a work and provide some basic information that might be missing. Naturally, if a catalog on a rare book is being reduced in content today, to fit the time and money squeeze, it is hardly surprising that the networks have placed even greater restrictions on what and how much can be stored on each item. The following figures show a regular MARC format, with a brief explanation of some of the basic fields, followed by examples of rare books listed in OCLC and how they approach the problem of cataloging each.[12]

## FIGURE 4   MARC Format Explanation

(1) Fixed field data.
(2) LC classification number assigned by local library, in Field 90 (as this would have been found in Field 50 if assigned by LC directly).
(3) 100 field, author.
(4) Indicating this will be an automatic added entry.
(5) 245 field contains body of the entry, title statement.
(6) 250 edition.
(7) 260 field, publication (imprint) data.
(8) 300 field, physical description.
(9) (c) MARC subfield code.
(10) 500 field, Notes (N.B., most printers cannot half-space, or ± (though on the screen this is done properly) and thus in Figure 8, line 10, of Paradise Lost this should appear as: pi$^2$ A-2V$^4$ (-2V2.3 ±pi$^2$)--corrected signature).
(11) 600s--tracings begin, Subject added entries.
(12) 700s--added entries.
(13) 800s--Series added entries.

## FIGURE 5   Oliver Twist

```
Screen 1 of 2
NO HOLDINGS IN VDB - FOR HOLDINGS ENTER dh DEPRESS DISPLAY RECD SEND
 OCLC: 12085927    Rec stat: n Entrd: 850528       Used: 850528
Type: a Bib lvl: m Govt pub:  Lang:  eng Source: d Illus:
Repr: Enc lvl: I Conf pub: O Ctry: enk Dat tp: q M/F/B:  10
Indx: O Mod rec: Festschr: O Cont:
Desc: a Int lvl: Dates: 1837,1929
 1 010
 2 040    BAT c BAT
 3 090    PZ3.D55 b 01    (2)
 4 090      b      (4)
 5 049    VDBB
 6 100 10 Dickens, Charles, d 1812-1870. w In    (3)
 7 240 10 Oliver Twist
 8 245 10 Oliver Twist or, The parish boy's progress / c by Charles Dickens  (5)
 9 250    Second edition.    (6)
10 260 0  Liverpool : b Published by the proprietors of the Bon Marchbe, in    (7)
Basnett Street, c [18--?].    (9)
11 300    112 p. : c 22 cm.    (8)
12 500    "The "B.M." edition of the standard works, published at one
penny."
13 500    Original printed green paper wrappers with portrait of Dickens on    (10)
front.

Screen 2 of 2
14 500    Edition statement from p. [1] of cover.
```

## FIGURE 6   Les Essais de Montaigne

```
Screen 1 of 2
NO HOLDINGS IN VDB - FOR HOLDINGS ENTER dh DEPRESS DISPLAY RECD SEND
 OCLC: 11057626     Rec Stat: n Entrd: 840815        Used: 840815
Type: a Bib lvl: m Govt pub:   Lang:  fre Source: d Illus:
 Repr:  Enc lvl: I Conf pub: O Ctry: fr Dat tp: s M/F/B: 10
 Indx: O Mod rec:  Festschr: O Cont:
 Desc:  Int lvl:  Dates: 1595.
  1 010
  2 040     VA@ c VA@
  3 090      b
  4 049     VDBB
  5 100 10 Montaigne, Michel de. d 1533-1592.
  6 245 14 Les essais de Michel sei-gnevr de Montaigne.
  7 250     Edition novvelle, b trovvee apres le deceds de l' autheur, reueuhe
& augmentbee par luy d' vn tiers qu' aux precedentes impressions.
  8 260 0  A Paris, b Chez Abel L' Angelier, au premier pilier de la grande
salle du Palais. (1595) Avec privilege, c (1595)
  9 300     (12) p. ., 523, [1] p. c 33 cm.
 10 500     Signatures: aD, eD, iD, A-ZF, Aa-VvF, XxD,
Aaa-SssF, Ttt-VvvD.

 Screen 2 of 2
 11 500     Errors in paging: pages 87, 88, 92 numbered 96, 97 and 76: 2d
group of numbers p. 59, 176-7 numbered 56, 178, and 179.
 12 500     "Essais de Michel de Montaigne.  Livre troisiesme." paged
separately.
 13 500     Head and tail pieces: initials.
 14 500     Edited by Marie de Gournay.--Brunet, 1838 ed., v. 3, p. 279.
 15 700 10 Gournay, Marie de Jars de, d d. 1645, e ed.
```

        *Although the French accents appear correctly on the screen, most
        printers are not equipped with them.

## FIGURE 7   Paradise Lost

```
 Screen 1 of 2
NO HOLDINGS IN VDB - FOR HOLDINGS ENTER dh DEPRESS DISPLAY RECD SEND
 OCLC: 10802614     Rec stat: c Entrd: 840604        Used: 840604
Type: a Bib lvl: m Govt pub:   Lang:  eng Source: d Illus:
 Repr:  Enc lvl: I Conf pub: O Ctry: enk Dat tp: s M/F/B: 10
 Indx: O Mod rec:  Festschr: O Cont:
 Desc: a Int lvl:  Dates: 1667,
  1 010
  2 040     IXa c IXA
  3 090     PR3560 b 1667
  4 090      b
  5 049     VDBB
  6 100 10 Milton, John, d 1608-1674.
  7 245 10 Paradise lost. : b A poem written in ten books / c by John
Miltonn.
  8 260 0  London : b Printed, and are to be sold by Peter Parker ... and by
Robert Boulter ... and Matthias Walker .... c 1667.
  9 300     [344] p. : c 19 cm. (4to)
 10 500     Signatures: piBA-2VD(-2V2.3 +piB)
 11 500     Head-pieces and initials.
 12 500     The first leaf (pi1) is blank.

 Screen 2 of 2
 13 500     For a description of the four issues of the first edition see:
Amory, Hugh. "Things unattempted yet: a bibliography of the first edition of
Paradise lost" in The Book collector, v. 32, no. 1 (spring 1983), p. 41-66.
 14 510 4  Amory H. First ed. of Paradise lost, c 1b
 15 510 4  Wing c M2136
 16 510 4  Grolier. Wither to Prior, c 599
```

FIGURE 8   Epistola Christoforia Colom

```
Screen 1 of 2
NO HOLDINGS IN VDB - FOR HOLDINGS ENTER dh DEPRESS DISPLAY RECD SEND
 OCLC: 10539549     Rec stat: n Entrd: 840320        Used: 840410
Type: a Bib lvl: m Govt pub:  Lang:  lat Source: d Illus:
 Repr:   Enc lvl: I Conf pub: O Ctry: it Dat tp: s M/F/B: 10
 Indx: O Mod rec:  Festschr: O Cont:
Desc: a Int lvl:  Dates: 1493.
 1 010
 2 040     FKS c FKS
 3 041 1   lat h spa
 4 043     nw ----
 5 090     E116.1 b 1493
 6 090      b
 7 049     VDBB
 8 100 10 Columbus, Christopher.
 9 245 10 Epistola Christofori Colom : cui etas nostra multu[m] debet : de
Insulis Indie supra Gangem nuper inve[n]tis.  b Ad quas perq[ui] rendas octauo
antea mense auspeciis [et] ere inuictissemo[rum] Ferna[n]di [et] Helisabet
Hispania[rum] Requ[m] missus ruerat : ad magnificum d[o]m[i]n[u]m. Gabrielem
Sanchis eorundem serenissimor[um] Regum Tesaurariu[m] missa...
10 260 0  [Rome : b Stephan Plannck, c after 29 April 1493]

Screen 2 of 2
11 300    [4] leaves : c 21 cm.
12 500    Caption title: usually cited : Epistola de insulis nuper inventis.
13 500    Translated from the original Spanish by Leander di Cosco.
14 500    Second edition. cf. Church, E.D. Discovery, v. 1, no. 56.
15 500    Without pagination, signature-marks or catch-words: 33 lines to
the full page.
16 500    Goff C758.
17 650 0  America x Discovery and exploration x Spanish.
18 700 10 Sanchez, Gabriel.
19 700 10 Cosco, Leandro di.
20 740 01 Epistola de insulis nuper inventis.
```

As the distribution of machine-readable computerized catalog information really began only in 1969 when the Library of Congress started issuing its MARC format, the network distribution systems have achieved much in some respects and little in others. The MARC format began with its current English language cataloging and within nine years had included all Roman alphabet languages. But the means for coordinating the distribution, the provision for the necessary technical, administrative, and legal work really began when OCLC (Ohio College Library Center) was created in 1971, to bring catalog data into each of its member libraries with a simple keyboard operation. It caught on quickly, and today, of the cataloging networks—RLG, WLN, SOLINET, CLASS, NELINET, AMIGOS (which uses the OCLC systems as its network resource for bibliographical systems)—OCLC remains the largest.[13]

Since 1971 great changes have taken place, not only in the technological field, but also in the administrative structures and goals.[14] Stanford University had its own system, BALLOTS, but when it was taken over by the RLG (Research Libraries Group), it assumed the acronym RLIN (Research Libraries Information Network) and focused on a limited number of research libraries. In 1975 it began to include other libraries and to modernize its system, so that by 1981 its clustered file design had streamlined its operations. Perhaps one of the weakest points of all the networks has been their lack of real interest in acquiring the catalogs of special collections. One of the great criticisms of OCLC was that though one could search a work by author, title, author-title, by its LC number, its ISBN, by the control number used by a particular network, and CODEN.[15] a work could not be located by "subject," which was a severe handicap, and thus when RLIN was established it did happily offer that alternative search ability.

But today all the systems are in a state of nearly frenzied change, including NELINET, the New England Library Information Network, in Wellesley, Massachusetts; CLASS, in San Jose, run by the California Library Authority for Systems and Services; SOLINET, the Southeastern Library Network, in Atlanta; AMIGOS, located in Dallas; and WLN, the Washington Library Network, in Olympia, but most of these do not provide online computer services to their members directly from the central offices.[16] Many of the changes have brought strong criticisms from individual libraries and local library groups as well. For instance, in 1978 OCLC became a different legal entity, OCLC, Inc., which immediately decided to drop all individual library members; hereafter a library could join only by forming a local network with other libraries. Similarly, RLG reformed in 1978, resulting in the decision to move its computers from the East coast to Stanford, although this resulted in the loss of several individual members, including Harvard. This loss came as a double blow to the group, which lost a large section of its database, as well as substantial financial support of its former members. RLIN is now weakened further by the fact that its acquisitions module is still limited to Stanford University Libraries.[17]

There are other problems concerning the networks, so far as the curator of rare books and manuscripts is concerned. Several rare book libraries do not belong to any of the networks, and of those that do, many do not enter all their holdings, and those which have been entered are at different cataloging levels.[18] Of the libraries that do belong, most do not belong to more than one network, so that if the institution has access to OCLC, it will not know what RLIN might have.[19] Thus, important materials may not be cataloged at all, or else are in a competing network to which you may not have access. Furthermore, special collections departments entering information into OCLC and other databases must conform to the network's format and restrictions on how much and what type of material is permitted. Also, some of the rare materials entered have been distorted through shortened titles, misspellings (especially of foreign languages), and an awkward ability to cope with foreign accent marks and alphabets.

Another problem not easily resolved and upon which it is difficult to obtain a consensus, is that of cataloging levels for rare books and manuscripts in computerized systems. Dr. Lawrence J. McCrank, head of the Department of Rare Books and Special Collections at Indiana State University suggests the following levels.[20]

1. Institution or repository description for directory information with access from broad, standardized subject descriptors such as form, place, and date of materials.
2. Collection or record-group and series description with uniform and inferred titles, name authority control, etc.
3. Short-title cataloging or inventory control, i.e., enumerative bibliography, which provides content analysis of the aggregate description at level 2.
4. Item level cataloging according to AACR2 using MARC as well as the standard archival data elements for description of books and manuscripts.
5. Descriptive bibliographic cataloging for rare books according to the L.C. Manual; similar format and set of descriptive standards could be devised for diplomatic and codicological description.
6. Advanced descriptive cataloging and manuscript description going beyond levels 4-5 by extensive notes, recording of variants, and using non-fixed length and repeatable fields in MARC to create full records (including conservation information, appraisal, etc., tied into a collection management system).

7. Full-text retrieval for edited materials, using optical scanning and laser-print delivery systems.
8. Facsimile retrieval for unedited material through reprographics, holographic and videodisc technology.
9. Document retrieval in actuality, whenever surrogation cannot satisfy user's needs.
10. Retrieval at the lower levels plus contextual information for collateral searching relating to content analysis, forensic and internal evidence, variants and collations, perhaps with linkage to on-line reference systems for retrieval of secondary and tertiary citations.

McCrank suggests that rare book catalogers use Level 5 as their standard, while bibliographers and those interested in textual exegesis attain Level 6. At the present time 47% of all rare books cataloged approach the AACR2 level, 39.8% reach Level 5 or the L.C. standard, and 13.3% attain Level 6 cataloging with expanded notes and possible detailed transcription and/or collation.[21]

There is growing pressure for higher standards, for an acceptable code for all library databases, but the Library of Congress seems to be playing less of a role in this. Because many rare book collections have not yet been entered—partially or entirely—and as a result of some inaccurate entries, it remains the task of each curator to acquire the knowledge of holdings of other libraries much as his or her predecessors traditionally have, by much reading and searching. What may possibly emerge out of all this is one central rare book network, providing services for all libraries, or at least an organization which will help make available knowledge of holdings to scholars which they might otherwise have missed, and perhaps something along the lines of UTOPIA, or the way manuscripts are now registered with the National Union Catalogue. For instance, I recently discovered several dozen first editions of works at the Hunt Institute on European colonial explorations. These works have never been published in a catalog, the Institute does not belong to a network and no effective steps have been taken to inform scholars of their existence. If a single national rare book network could encourage such libraries to disclose their holdings, it would prove most valuable to scholars and librarians.

Another shortcoming of most reference collections in special collections departments in the United States is a general lack of interest, on the part of curators, in the catalogs and holdings of rare works in most of the European countries. The Italian catalogs, for example, are rarely represented, though they are immensely valuable, and yet what is the likelihood of Rumanian, Czech, West and East German, French, or Yugoslav rare book entries' being entered into an international network?

Perhaps the most useful aspect of the networks as applied to rare books and manuscripts is their ability to indicate rapidly the location of various editions. But even this is limited in effectiveness by the grossly incomplete holdings of such databanks and by the failure to take into consideration the major European holdings of rare works. Nevertheless, the move to enter rare works into the databanks of the various networks appears to be inevitable in a society that is daily becoming more and more reliant upon computers for everything. Perhaps one day in the distant future, curators may be able to count upon such computerized services with some assurance of factual reliability and completeness.

## References

1. Ronald B. McKerrow, *An Introduction to Bibliography for Literary Students* (Oxford: Clarendon Press, 1928), p. 5, and Fredson Bowers, *Principles of Bibliographical Description* (Princeton, N.J.: Princeton University Press, 1949, renewed 1977), p. viii.
2. Bowers, p. vii.
3. *Bibliographic Description of Rare Books. Rules Formulated Under AACR2 and ISBD(A) for the Descriptive Cataloging of Rare Books and Other Special Printed Materials* (Washington, D.C.: Library of Congress, 1981), pp. 55; 58. See also, Paul Shaner Dunkin, *How to Catalog a Rare Book* (Chicago: American Library Association, 1951).
4. Allan Stevenson, comp., *Catalogue of Botanical Books in the Collection of Rachel McMasters Miller Hunt,* Vol. II, Part II, *Printed Books 1701-1800* (Pittsburgh: The Hunt Botanical Library, 1961).
5. See Bohdan S. Wynar, with the assistance of Arlene Taylor Dowell and Jeanne Osborn, *Introduction to Cataloging and Classification,* 6th ed. (Littleton, Colo.: Libraries Unlimited, 1980).
6. Brunet (1780-1867) published the *Manuel du Librarie et de l'Amateur de Livres* in 1810. See under Brunet, in Ch. 11, Reference Works.
7. Bohdan Wynar, p. 35.
8. Roderick Cave, *Rare Book Librarianship,* 2nd ed. (London: Clive Bingley, 1982), p. 67.
9. *Ibid.*, p. 68.

10. *Ibid.*, p. 70. Cave is referring to Stevenson's *Catalogue of Botanical Books.*

11. Stevenson, pp. 64-65. Bowers provides examples in the appendixes of his book (cited above), but Stevenson is even more complete.

12. Courtesy of OCLC, Inc., with author's explanation.

13. See Susan K. Martin's study, *Library Networks, 1981-82* (White Plains, N.Y.: Knowledge Industry Publications, Inc., 1981). The number of articles on networks grows annually, but references to rare books are infrequent. See also: ALA, Association of Colleges and Research Libraries. Rare Books & MSS Section. Standards Committee. "Relator Terms for Rare Book, Manuscript, and Special Collections Cataloguing," *College and Research Libraries News,* No. 8 (Sept. 1980), 238–39. R.C. Alston and R.A. Christophers, "Bibliographical Control of Older Books: Machine-Readable Cataloguing and Early Printed Books," *International Cataloguing,* 8, Nos. 1, 2 (Jan.–April 1979), 9–12, 16–18. Terry Belanger and S.P. Davis, "Rare Book Cataloguing and Computers—I," *AB Bookman's Weekly,* 63 (Feb. 5, 1979), 1955–56. Terry Belanger, "Rare Book Cataloguing and Computers—II; *AB Bookman's Weekly,* 65 (Jan. 14, 1980), 187–88. D.A. Cargille, "Variant Edition Cataloguing in OCLC: Input or Adapt?" *Library Resources and Technical Services,* 27, No. 1 (Jan. 1982), 47–51. R.P. Holley and D. Flecker, "Processing OCLC and MARC Subscription Tapes at Yale University," *Journal of Library Automation,* 12 (Mar. 1979), 88–91. "Kansas Receives Grant to Catalogue Rare Books," *Wilson Library Bulletin,* 54 (Jan. 1980), 281. P.C. Knight, "Cataloguing with OCLC and RLIN: A Comparative Analysis," *North Carolina Libraries,* 38 (Summer 1980), 430–36. See also the various manuals available on processing online data, e.g. *On-line Systems Manuscripts Format, C80-7* (Columbus, Ohio: OCLC, 1980).

14. See Barbara Markuson and Blanche Woolls, eds., *Networks for Networkers: Critical Issues in Cooperative Library Development* (New York: Neal-Schuman Publishers, 1980).

15. CODEN, used for scientific abstracting and indexing.

16. Martin, p. 3.

17. Martin criticizes this, p. 5.

18. Lawrence J. McCrank, "The Bibliographic Control of Rare Books: Phased Cataloguing, Descriptive Standards, and Costs," *Cataloging & Classifying Quarterly,* 5, No. 1 (Fall 1984), 37–38.

19. According to figures given by McCrank, OCLC has records of 3,952,000 volumes of rare books held by its members, while RLIN reports 3,641,536 volumes. The 1982 survey of book librarians in institutions belonging to IRLA, ARL, and ACRL indicates that only 10.7% still prepared rare book bibliographical control manually, while 82% of those institutions responding to the survey belonged to OCLC, and 17.4% to ARLIN (McCrank, pp. 36, 37, 38).

20. *Ibid.*, pp. 37–38.
21. *Ibid.*, p. 42. McCrank quotes current cost estimates to catalog rare books at Level 4, varying from $4.65 to $227 per unit; however, he also lists average cataloging costs per unit by geographical region in this country, ranging from $11.49 in the Pacific Northwest to $57.81 per unit in the Middle Atlantic States. It should be pointed out that these costs exclude any detailed forensic examination that might be required to prove the authenticity of a document. For further reading on this subject, see Lawrence J. McCrank and Jay Elvove, "The Mt. Angel Abbey Rare Book and Manuscript Project Revisited: A Case Study in Automated Cataloging and Publishing," *Sixth International Conference of Computers and Humanities* (Rockville, Md.: Computer Science Press, 1983), pp. 415–30; Nedra L. Kaynes, *Unit time/cost study in the Cataloging Unit* (Tucson, Ariz.: Technical Services, Public Library, 1978) also found in *ERIC Report* ED-194091; Robin Alston and M.J. Jannetta, *Bibliography, Machine-readable Cataloging, and the ESTC* (London: British Library, 1978); and Albert Gruijs and Per Holager, "A Plan for Computer Assisted Codicography of Medieval Manuscripts," *Quarendo,* 11 (1981), pp. 95–119.

# 4

# Conservation and Preservation

It is with the greatest reluctance that library administrators are beginning to face the unpleasant fact that books and archival materials are not indestructible. When $100,000 is spent on new monographs and serials, there is something on the shelf to display for the outlay of funds. When a leather binding needs to be treated with a coating of potassium lactate, or a torn leaf needs to be mended, or a book has to be dusted or treated for deacidification, the volume rarely looks very different after treatment, at least to the untrained eye. Nevertheless, conservation and preservation must be undertaken. If the Golden Gate Bridge were not painted continually to fight the sea air erosion, it would collapse into the sea. If books and manuscripts are not maintained, they become illegible and gradually disintegrate.

Despite the great effort necessary to deal with the seemingly uncontrollable conservation/preservation problem, the subject is at last beginning to receive attention. For instance, Notre Dame University's bindery budget is theoretically, to set aside ten percent for preservation, although in fact that figure is halved. Thanks to such organizations as the Association of Research Libraries, and their numerous publications, the librarian and library administrator are now constantly being reminded of their obligations. The ARL has recently stated:

During the last decade, libraries have increasingly recognized that their collections are seriously endangered by a combination of damaging environmental conditions, improper handling, and the declining quality of materials themselves. It has been estimated that a third of the materials in research library collections have reached a state of deterioration that makes further use almost impossible, and as many as half may be unusable by the end of the century.[1]

60

Notre Dame, like so many other universities, will provide hundreds of thousands of dollars for football uniforms, equipment, and coaches, but reduce its preservation budget of a few thousand dollars by half. The ARL points out that one of the many problems is simply the lack of common standards or traditions of practice, for in reality conservation and preservation comprise an area fully understood and appreciated by just a handful of people. The series published by the Office of Management Studies of the ARL is the more valuable because each publication is the result of a survey made by its members. For instance, in March 1980, forty member libraries reported having conducted a formal preservation study or at least a needs assessment, twenty-eight had adopted planning or policy documents, and another fifty-eight reported operating an active preservation program with an average of three full- or part-time staff members to aid with preservation and conservation functions. Nineteen libraries indicated their intent to implement such a program within the next five years. To the credit of ARL, they are continuing their work in this field.[2]

The fact remains, however, that the vast majority of library collections—special or not—are generally out of control so far as preservation is concerned. The reasons for this are numerous. Unlike older, more established libraries, such as those in Western Europe, where preservation and conservation are an integral aspect of every important library collection, most American libraries are "new," and conservation and preservation lack traditional acceptance and understanding. This in turn reflects an interesting psychological valuation in relegating "books" to a category below, say, computers and technology in general, or even football. American library administrators prefer to spend their money more visibly. The vast majority of library schools do not teach a single course on conservation or preservation, and apart from such institutions as Columbia or Johns Hopkins, programmed conservation-preservation courses are ignored. Indeed, it is only now that the first graduate degree in the administration of this subject is at last being introduced at Columbia. A significant factor is that, except for specialists in conservation and preservation, like Rutherford Rogers of Yale, most American library administrators and directors are simply ignorant of the problems in this area.

Some libraries, on the other hand, are beginning to recognize just how devastatingly pervasive and costly this ignorance is, and what a legacy we have consequently been left. Thus, when the University of Kansas made a partial study of its Spencer Collection and found that fifty percent of its 150,000 volumes needed "some kind of conservation treatment, some simple, some complex," they were so alarmed that they followed this up with a fuller survey of all their collections and the results they found to be "disheartening," the overseeing committee concluding that the results more than "justified in calling the problem severe."[3] They based their study on the age of the books and the condition of the paper and came up with the following statistics: They found that the condition of the paper in 530,770 volumes was "strong" (the vast majority of those books were published within the last twenty-five years), and that 397,551 contained paper in a "weakening" condition and 138,052 in "weakened" condition, while in the fourth category of deterioration, referred to as "brittle," 112,718 qualified, and in the fifth category, they found that the paper of 31,187 volumes was beyond brittle, simply "broken." "It is absolutely predictable that as our books turn seventy-five years old their paper will have become so embrittled that they will be unusable."[4] Kansas calculated that as of 1975, thirteen percent of their total university collection was brittle, and that in three-quarters of a century that figure would be doubled.[5]

The figure of seventy-five years seems to others to be entirely too optimistic. The Barrows Laboratory estimated that ninety-seven percent of non-fiction books published in this country between 1900 and 1939 had a useful life expectancy of fifty years or less, while a former chief preservation officer of the Library of Congress, Frazer Poole, estimates that thirty to thirty-five years would be a more accurate estimation of the expectancy of present day book papers![6]

Some libraries conduct inhouse investigations of their physical holdings, while others contract the services of outside consultants to make a complete study of the library's conservation and preservation needs, which frequently necessitates going into considerable detail pinpointing minute problems which are causing the destruction of materials. George M. Cunha, Director of the New England Document Conservation Center, prepared just such a study for the University of Utah Libraries. Cunha's report included drawing up a list of priority items needed to ensure the proper care of books, down to such protective devices as filters against ultraviolet rays, light monitoring, temperature and humidity controls (for instance, he discovered that in some places the humidity fell fifty percent below the recommended level), polyester encapsulation of documents, proper boxing instructions, and so on. Columbia University estimated that 1.5 million volumes of its holdings were considered to be in "an advanced state of deterioration," which at an average cost of $22.80 per volume to rectify, would require the outlay of $34,213,900.[7] Stanford University Libraries, attempting to anticipate their book deterioration problems by 1995, reckoned that it would cost their university $82,500,000 to save their collections![8]

Now the interesting aspect of the above surveys is that they are not concerned primarily with rare or special holdings, but with the average problem of deterioration in any good research library. Though the estimate of $22.80 to restore each volume would ideally cover the cost of binding, shipping, and paperwork for a book in the open stacks, such a figure would not begin to deal with the cost of conserving, preserving, and repairing rare books and manuscripts.

Many libraries have simple regulations for classifying the types of bindings expected from binderies for works intended for the regular research stacks, but make no attempt to match or restore the original binding or keep the same sort of style or quality.[9] With rare books, however, that sort of cavalier attitude is out of the question. When Norman J. Shaffer served as chief of the preservation office of the Library of Congress, he attempted to assess the *total* requirements for restoration and preservation of the Library's rare and valuable collections, estimating that "12,000 man-years of work" would be needed.[10]

We are frequently dealing with collections worth a minimum of $50 million and yet do little or nothing to protect our investment. The underlying reasons are twofold: time and money. Each volume is a separate problem, and a costly, time-consuming affair even if trained personnel are available.[11] A broken spine, dry rot, migrating acidification, water damage, worming, loose lacings, torn pages, maps, and tip-ins—all have to be faced as individual problems, and yet all may be present in a single volume.

All curators of special collections know when they accept their post that conservation and preservation will be a constant problem. If a special collections department has not had a complete survey within the past few years of the state of preservation of the collection, then the curator must plan to make such a survey as soon as possible. If the library contains tens of thousands of rare items, it may be necessary to go beyond the resources of the institution and call upon those of the New England Document Conservation Center, for example. (Unfortunately, the Barrows Laboratories, which also did preservation work, have closed their doors permanently). The planning document first assesses the general situation and then establishes the objectives and priorities needed for a plan of action, and this will certainly include a close monitoring of every volume on a regular basis. The library will no doubt prepare a special form listing various items which will be checked off against each volume, all in addition to the usual bibliographic data. These will in turn ultimately form a permanent historical reference file for each item. The checklist prepared in Figure 1 could be used as a model.

The necessary steps for taking corrective action will have to be determined and then a code applied to explain what type of action must be taken. To have an effective conservation/preservation program, certain elementary steps must be taken and certain basic elements present:

1. An assessment of the physical state of the materials and surroundings must be made.
2. A plan for correcting the problems of each item must be drafted, with a list of priorities.
3. A conservation/preservation staff and workshop must be adequate in size to meet the needs of the department.
4. A policy on microfilming must be established and consistently applied.
5. A decision must be made as to what types of repairs will be made in-house (rare books, maps, and manuscripts only), and what kinds of repairs must be done by specialists elsewhere.
6. Adequate storage must be provided for every type of material (books, manuscripts, letters, maps, drawings, microfilm, etc.).
7. A plan to meet various emergencies (fire, flood) must be prepared.

## ASSESSMENT AND PLANNING

That many universities and institutions are now aware of the necessity of preparing assessment and planning reports is attested to by the reports issued by the University of Notre Dame, the University of Virginia, the University of Wisconsin at Madison, the University of Kansas, Arizona State University, Duke University, the University of Utah, the California State Library Authority, and the Library of Congress.

Informed, well-reasoned, long-term strategies must be developed in order to insure the continued existence and usefulness of our collections. To achieve this end, a standing Committee for Preservation has been established. The initial task of the Committee will be to investigate the scope of the problem of deteriorating materials within the University Library and to educate itself with respect to the variety of available solutions.[12]

This statement made by the University of Virginia in February 1980 is fairly typical of the attitude and concerns of most universities. The University of Connecticut Library's Preservation Office went so far as to list ten objectives, including the establishment and implementation of a comprehensive preservation program for all library materials, the formulation of policies and procedures for the proper care of the various collections, the examination and monitoring of the library's environmental conditions on a regular basis, the development and implementation of inhouse preservation treatments, the development and implementation of policies and procedures for handling materials of permanent research value which are in unusable condition, the developing of a testing and quality control program for all library materials, the training of staff in care and handling of library materials, the creation of a research center for conservation and preservation information, the preparation and coordination of budget estimates and requests for the preservation of the collection, and finally, the preparation of procedures for protecting materials during emergencies or disasters.[13]

More detailed planning documents have been prepared elsewhere, including the California Library Authority for Systems and Services, whose assistant director, J. Michael Bruer, produced a fifty-one-page guideline for the entire state, entitled *Toward a California Document Conservation Program*.[14] This document is replete with short- and long-range objectives, calling for training and research planning, the case for regional conservation centers, while "the emphasis in this paper is on multi-national facilities dealing with a full range of conservation issues on a state-wide or interstate basis."[15] Since the writing of that report, eighteen western states have formed the Western States Materials Conservation Project, sponsored by the Western Council of State Libraries, Inc.[16] Its aims are:

1.  To develop an informed cadre of conservation conscious librarians, archivists, and manuscript curators in each Western Council state

### FIGURE 1　Rare Books, Manuscripts Repairs—Order Authorization

Call No. _____

Name of Special Collection _____

Author _____

Title _____

Place Published _____ Publisher _____

Year Published _____

Rare _____　　　　Very Rare _____　　　Only Known Copy _____

Purchase Price _____ Appraised Value _____

In-house repairs? _____

To be sent out (if so to whom) _____

Estimate of costs _____

Urgent, return by _____ Not Urgent, return by _____

Type of Material:

   1.　Book(s)___ no. of vols.___ no. of pgs.___ size:___ cm. x ___ cm.

   2.　Pamphlet _____ no. of pages _____ size: _____ cm. x _____ cm.

   3.　MS. ___ no. of vols. ___ no. of pgs. ___ size: ___ cm. x ___ cm.

   4.　Letters(s) ___ no. of leaves/pages ___ size: _____ cm. x ___ cm.

   5.　Map(s) _____ size: _____ cm. x _____ cm.

   6.　Engraving, print, illustration (indicate) _____
      Size: _____ cm. x _____ cm.

   7.　Newspaper(s) _____ no. of pages ____ size: ____ cm. x ____ cm.

   8.　Official document (describe) _____ size: ____ cm. x ____ cm.

   9.　Other _____

Date this work recommended for repairs _____ by whom _____

Date sent out for repairs _____ Date returned _____

Final Cost _____ Paid by Account No. _____

Remarks by conservator: e.g., book's delicate condition requires restricted use, recommends microfilming.

Authorization to repair (Curator and Date) _____

Type of Repairs/Work Required:

A. Binding:

1. Original binding: leather (type and color) _____
   paper _____ cloth _____ other _____

2. Clean _____ Oil _____

3. Spine: loose _____ broken or cracked _____ detached _____

4. Front cover: loose ____ broken or cracked ____ detached _____
   Front cover: repair corner(s) _____ Warped _____

5. Repair inner joints _____ new pastedowns _____

6. Repair binding recommended _____ not recommended _____
   Restore binding recommended _____ not recommended _____

7. Repair headband _____

8. Back cover: loose _____ broken or cracked ____ detached _____
   Back cover: repair corner(s) _____ Warped _____

9. Repair inner joints _____ new pastedowns _____

10. Bookplate needed _____ Quires, sewing _____

11. Requires new cover or binding (indicate type) _____

12. Mylar encapsulation _____ Other _____

B. Text:

1. Page(s) or margin(s) torn, pp. _____

2. Page(s) loose or detached, pp. _____

3. Page(s) missing, pp. _____

4. Tip-ins: loose _____ torn _____ missing _____

5. Maps: loose _____ torn _____ missing _____

6. Illustrations: loose _____ torn _____ missing _____

7. Acid migration, pp. _____

8. Water damage, pp. _____

9. Pages to be cleaned _____

10. Pages to be: trimmed _____ cut _____

11. Other

who are committed to, and will work for, conservation solutions on a local, state, regional, and national basis;
2. To survey, and report on, conservation issues, constraints, potential solutions, priorities, alternatives, available resources, and the feasibility of a variety of coordinated conservation activities in the West;
3. To develop, by consensus and in priority sequence, a cooperative, coordinated conservation action plan for the West;
4. To plan, as appropriate, implementation of the conservation action plan developed.[17]

The report concluded that the members must concentrate in three general areas: information and education; conservation services; and standards, research, and legislation. Awareness of conservation/preservation problems is growing on state, regional, and even national levels. The age of hit-or-miss book and manuscript preservation is coming to an end at last.

It is not surprising that a national program for libraries should be considered, and a few years ago the Library of Congress drafted a seven-page document outlining "A National Preservation Program for Libraries." It called for exactly that, a national preservation program—not unlike the California report—which emphasized storage problems of rare materials (even the possibility of "storage at low-temperature in warehouse-type structures or in underground caves") and strongly suggested that this type of solution "offers the most economical and feasible method of preserving these materials for indefinite periods of time."[18] It also stressed careful evaluation of the use of microfilming of valuable works and their storage. The study suggested that one of the most effective and productive programs would be the establishment of "national conservation programs" by the Library of Congress, through "one or more regional conservation centers,"[19] which could be housed at universities and would serve as "national workshops" where librarians could be sent for training in the art of conservation. Also proposed were the preparation of training films to be disseminated to libraries, and the provision of emergency salvation teams. The Library of Congress paper also recommended that the copyright law be amended to include the submission of three, not two, copies of each published book, the third to become part of the "National Preservation Collection" to be stored under ideal conditions. It also called for a suitable record-keeping center and the establishment of national microfilming facilities for the preservation and use of deteriorating library copies. It advocated mounting a drive to persuade paper-makers to produce better, more durable paper for books. Finally, the report admitted that strong, long-term funding would be needed "to fund a sound program to preserve the national heritage in the nation's libraries,"[20] although it stopped short of suggesting how or where such funding was to be provided.

What all these studies seem to agree upon is the need for more effective conservation laboratories and an increase in trained library personnel to cope with conservation and preservation. The problem of book deterioration can be handled effectively only by means of larger, cooperative ventures, whether by a group of regional universities, an interstate council, or on a national level, coordinated by the Library of Congress.

## CONSERVATION AND PRESERVATION

Repairs to rare books and manuscripts and bindings are frequently made in special library facilities. Before discussing the conservation/preservation workshop, however, we should define a few terms: "Preservation" refers to the action taken to retard, stop, or prevent deterioration, whereas "conservation" generally means maintaining in usable condition each item in the collection. "Restoration" means returning the deteriorated item as closely as possible to its original condition. The newer term, "information preservation," means taking the information from an original document and transferring it to another material, such as by reprinting or microfilming.

The size of the workshop depends upon the size of the library and the amount of financial support it receives. Jean Gunner at the Hunt Institute has an excellent workshop with a fairly representative array of tools and materials needed, but the use is limited by a small staff. Rutherford Rogers and David Weber suggest that a "typical" binding and preservation staff would comprise:

one Librarian II
one Librarian I or Supervising Assistant
two Senior Bookbinders for in-house work
two bindery preparation clerks
five library assistants for finishing tasks (plating, tagging, marking, and pocketing)[21]

Bonnie Jo Cullison, preservation librarian at the Newberry, has four assistant conservators, exclusive of John Robinson's bindery section with his eight assistants. Preservation has such a high priority at the Newberry that one of the three special advisors to the vice president of the Library is George A. Poole III, the curator of rare books.[22] Columbia University's preservation department consists of four units: the bindery, materials processing, the reprography laboratory, and the preservation records office—staffed by twenty-three full-time members, six of whom are professional and supervisory staff.

One of the first decisions of the head of the conservation/preservation department is what is to be done by the inhouse bindery and what goes to the commercial binder. At Columbia, for instance, almost all paperback material and pamphlets are sent directly to commercial vendors. But any decision on binding rare books is generally difficult and frequently time-consuming. Rarely if ever will an attempt be made to replace say, a fifteenth century Italian binding. Is the book simply loose in its case, or is a board or spine broken? Is it better to secure the lacing and place the book, broken spine and all, in a specially designed box? Multiply these questions by thousands of volumes and one wonders how such large numbers of works are in fact produced. Rogers and Weber quoted some astonishing figures for annual production at their university library.[23]

Volumes sent outside for binding: 15,300
Volumes rebound internally: 4,000
Volumes repaired: 12,800
Volumes finished: 85,000

To decide on an outside commercial binder, Rogers and Weber compiled a list of questions which had to be applied first:

1. Are competitive prices maintained for comparable work?
2. Is the maximum turnaround time in the shop one month?
3. Will the binder provide special services (e.g., within one or two weeks) to expedite "rush" requests for reference works or books for the circulation reserve?
4. Is the size of the bindery sufficient to handle the university's work without fluctuating production volume?
5. Can transportation time from the bindery be limited to one-half work day for special recalls, and are deadlines met?

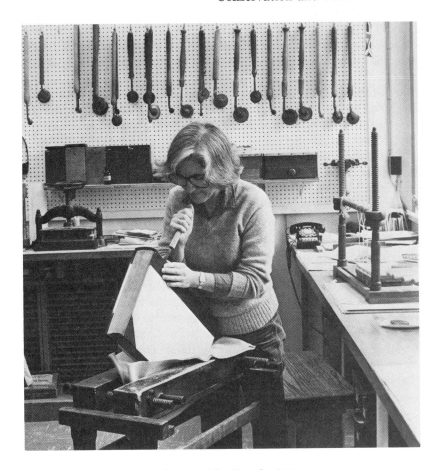

Jean Gunner of the Hunt Institute.

6. Is the bindery capable of providings bindings not only to meet national specifications but any variations on the theme?
7. Is the workmanship careful enough to save the maximum amount of the margin when sanding the spine for rebuilding or, once the book is rebound, can it be opened without splitting and tearing?
8. Are shipping and billing procedures reliable and efficient?
9. Can the binder provide occasional special requests (such as leather work, solander cases, and slipcases)?[24]

In short, is the commercial bindery of your choice large enough to handle a variety of jobs carefully, expeditiously, reliably, and at a reasonable cost? The fact remains that the binding problems posed by special collections cannot generally be met by commercial binderies, hence the need for special bindery and preservation laboratories, such as the New England Document Conservation Center, the Columbia inhouse workshop, or the varied and special abilities of a Jean Gunner at the Hunt Institute.

Certain rare books and manuscripts are so "rare" that one fears tampering with them at all, and occasionally librarians even discourage scholars from cutting the pages of a book, forgetting that one of the essential reasons for the existence of such libraries is to provide knowledge and information for their researchers. The rare books in question may have been bought at auction for some extraordinary figure, and naturally one does not wish to destroy the genuine qualities of that work. Binding is invariably discouraged, and worming not easily remedied. But sometimes rare books are damaged by natural catastrope, as by the terrible floods of Florence which so badly damaged tens of thousands of priceless works. R. S. Almagno, who worked with a team from the Vatican, tells of the tedious work of dismembering those books and washing them, page by page, and then resewing them. In 1980, a water main burst in the basement of Yale's Sterling Library, flooding priceless archives and manuscripts, which were saved only by shipping them immediately to previously designated deep-freeze centers, per their emergency plan.[25] The problem of migrating acid especially afflicts more recent works of the nineteenth and twentieth centuries. How is one to cope with this? As the spread of acid frequently begins with the tissue protecting a frontispiece or title page, one can start there. Insert an acid-free tip-in? Treat chemically? Use the deep-freeze technique? Different curators have different answers. Even something seemingly as simple as mending a torn page can cause a controversy. Should a special tape be applied, or Japanese tissue, or a new paste? Jean Gunner argues that no one but a trained conservator should make that judgment. The composition of the oil used to treat leather may vary; each curator has his or her own special formula. Should books be placed behind dust-free glass cases? How does one dust books? With a cloth or a vacuum? When it comes to rare books there is rarely a simple answer acceptable to all curators.

## ENVIRONMENT AND STORAGE

The storage of books, manuscripts, and archival records is perhaps less controversial than most subjects. Do you want wooden or metal shelves? Do you want glass-enclosed cases? Are you going to store letters in Hollinger boxes vertically or horizontally? The basics of storage are simple. Keep the materials in a dimly lit, dust-free area with controlled temperature and humidity (60°F and 50 percent humidity) in every room, every hour of the day.[26] The general rule of thumb is that for every ten degrees the temperature is dropped, the life of paper is doubled.

Wooden shelving is certainly more attractive and also more expensive than metal, but of course it is not fireproof. Metal shelving is ugly, but it cannot cause paint, stain, or varnish damage as wood can. The Hunt Institute recommends the use of non-glass enclosed shelves which can still be secured by some sort of metal covering, allowing air in and thereby preventing the books on the shelves from suffering from the embrittling hothouse effect caused by some glass-enclosed cases. Effective air filters should be installed, not only throughout the building but on the roof as well. Direct sunlight must be kept out, and a variety of anti-ultraviolet-ray devices can be employed inside and outside the building: ultraviolet filtering varnish, ultraviolet filtering film (as a solar screen), ultraviolet filtering sheet plastic; the absence of fluorescent lighting, the presence of photometers, etc.

Even the most dust-free environments have doors which permit the movement of air into the room; how often and in what manner books are to be dusted is debatable. Some curators like a cloth; others prefer jets of air. At the Library of Congress, vacuum dusting is preferred and probably best.


## PRACTICAL HANDBOOKS

Many libraries have their own handbooks and manuals on the care and preservation of rare books, manuscripts, letters, and archives, e.g., Columbia University's *Binding and Physical Treatment Handbook,* just as the libraries in the province of Québec use an excellent work by Alain Boucher entitled *Le Service de Préservation et de Réparation.*[27]

Three other works deserve special mention here not only because of their reasonable cost and availability, but also because they cover the full gamut of problems likely to be encountered in a special collection, and they explain simply and clearly—aided by excellent illustrations and photographs—how to cope with the issues at hand.

Bernard Middleton's *The Restoration of Leather Bindings,*[28] first published by the American Library Association in 1972, is still a basic work, enhanced by Aldren A. Watson's large and meticulous illustrations. The book includes a complete glossary of terms, describes workshops, tools, equipment, and materials, the cleaning of bindings, and the removal of the original spine. The author discusses resewing and its alternatives, gluing, rounding and backing, headbanding, back lining, preparing boards for rebacking, and then the rebacking process, repairing inner joints and replacing the original spine, repairing caps and outer joints without rebacking, repairing caoutchouc bindings, repairing corners (including the method of injecting paste into the board with a hypodermic syringe), the blending in of new endpapers, straightening of warped boards, rebinding old pasteboards, salvaging old sides, with a chapter on staining, aging, tooling, and refurbishing, and then the preparation of a record of repairs made to all works. The author includes a brief list of references. This excellent book cannot be praised highly enough.

Middleton's work on leather bindings is nicely supplemented by two other works: Carolyn Horton's well established *Cleaning and Preserving Bindings and Related Materials,*[29] and Carolyn Clark Morrow's more recent *Conservation Treatment Procedures.*[30] Horton's work is divided into three general sections: the preparation required prior to reconditioning a library (removing books, recording shelf positions, vacuuming, etc.), a section entitled "Sorting Books and Identifying Problems" (including labels, book jackets, various types of leather bindings, the inspection of cloth, paper, and vellum bindings, bookplates, enclosures, acid migration, tightening books in their cases, loose labels, etc.), and then the largest and most important part of the book, "Treatment" (of bookplates, tightening books in cases, coping with acid migration, cleaning maps, leaf repairs, etc.), followed by a glossary, lists of supplies and equipment, and a select bibliography.

Carolyn Clark Morrow's book is the most up-to-date work on the market. Following the useful introduction, the sections are "Book Repair Procedure" (tightening hinges of a cased book, new bookcloth spines with mounted original spines, recasing using the original cover, and applying a new cover), "Maintenance Procedures" (including pamphlet binding, pressboard binding, mending with Japanese paper and paste, and leather treatment), and "Protective Encasement Procedures" (covering, polyester film encapsulation, simple portfolios, four-flap portfolios, and the solander case). The book is completed by several useful appendixes icluding a "Standard Rate System for Measuring Productivity," a "Dexterity Test," and a glossary. This book is accompanied by a complete set of photographs illustrating each step of each procedure. One hopes the above works will soon be joined by one specializing in paper maintenance and repairs.

The problem unique to rare works—books, manuscripts, maps, or even paintings—is whether or not "restoration" of any type will add to or detract from the value and quality of the work. There is probably no general rule applicable to rare works which can guide the curator in the matter of restoration and repairs, except, perhaps, when in doubt, do not act. But this does not mean that one would refrain from consulting another expert in the field. The maintenance, repair, and restoration of rare printed works is an art, and thus it is the conservator, the artist, who must be consulted.

## References

1. *Planning for Preservation, SPEC Kit 66* (July-August 1980), ii. SPEC Kits are published by the Systems and Procedures Exchange Center, Association of Research Libraries, Office of Management Studies, Washington, D.C.
2. *Ibid.,* p. i.
3. "Report of Dean of Libraries' Committee on Conservation," University of Kansas, October, 1975, p. 2. This was reprinted in SPEC Kit 66.
4. *Ibid.*
5. *Ibid.*
6. "The Conservation and Preservation Program for the University Libraries at Stanford," Stanford University, January 1978. See also Frazer Poole's "Thoughts on the Conservation of Library Materials," in *Library and Archives* (Boston: Boston Athenaeum, 1972), p. 19.
7. Quoted in the Stanford Report of January 1978, "The Conservation and Preservation Program," p.1.
8. *Ibid.*
9. In fact some university libraries do lay down very strict binding requirements in terms of strength and durability of product, etc., but these do not apply to rare works. See, for example, "Minimum Specifications for Library Bindings," produced for the University of Connecticut.

10. "Preservation and Conservation Procedures and Philosophies Developed at the Library of Congress, Washington, D.C." prepared by Norman J. Shaffer and republished in SPEC Kit 66, p. 79 (p. 2 of the original document). According to other figures released by the Library of Congress in 1973, 40% of its 17 million volumes were even then "too brittle to be given to the user." See Karen Lee Shelly, "The Future of Conservation in Research Libraries," *Journal of Academic Libraries,* 1, No. 6 (Jan. 1976), 15.

11. *A National Preservation Program for Libraries* (Washington, D.C., Library of Congress, Office of the Assistant Director for Preservation, 1976), p. 3. In 1973 the Library of Congress estimated a cost of $24 just to microfilm "the average three hundred page volume," whereas to restore a book to "its original format" would cost 10 to 15 times as much.

12. "Charge to University Library Committee for Preservation," dated February 25, 1980, University of Virginia, quoted in SPEC Kit, p. 3.

13. "A Preservation Program: Proposal and Preservation Office Responsibilities," University of Connecticut, published in SPEC Kit 66, p. 18.

14. *Toward a California Document Conservation Program,* published on October 1, 1978, partly through funds administered by the California State Library.

15. *Ibid.,* p. 35.

16. Participating members in this project include: Alaska, Arizona, California, Colorado, Idaho, Iowa, Kansas, Montana, Nebraska, Nevada, New Mexico, North Dakota, Oklahoma, Oregon, South Dakota, Utah, Washington, and Wyoming.

17. *Ibid.,* see pp. 1-3, of the "Survey Report, Western States Materials Conservation Project," released in Denver, Colorado, on April 21, 1980.

18. *A National Preservation Program For Libraries.*

19. *Ibid.,* p. 6.

20. *Ibid.,* p. 7.

21. Rutherford D. Rogers and David C. Weber, *University Library Management* (New York: H.W. Wilson, 1971), p. 189.

22. *The Annual Report of the Newberry Library for the Year Ending June 30, 1982* (Chicago: Newberry Library, 1982), p. 13.

23. Rogers and Weber, p. 189.

24. *Ibid.,* p. 187.

25. *Report of the University Librarian, July 1980-June 1981.* This comprised the entire special issue of the *Bulletin of Yale University,* 78, No. 1 (January 1, 1982), 35-36.

26. These figures, somewhat lower than those applied in most libraries, are recommended by the Newberry. *The Annual Report of the Newberry,* 1982, p. 6.

27. Alain Boucher, *Le Service de Préservation et de Réparation* (2nd rev. ed.) (La Pocatière, Québec: Collège de Sainte-Anne-de-la-Pocatière, 1970).
28. Bernard C. Middleton, *The Restoration of Leather,* illustr. by Aldren A. Watson. Library Technology Program Publication 18. (Chicago: American Library Association, 1972).
29. Carolyn Horton, *Cleaning and Preserving Bindings and Related Materials,* illustr. by Aldren Watson. Library Technology Program Publication 12. (Chicago: American Library Association, 1967).
30. Carolyn Clark Morrow, *Conservation Treatment Procedures: A Manual of Step-by-Step Procedures for the Maintenance and Repair of Library Materials* (Littleton, Colo.: Libraries Unlimited, 1982).

# 5

## Public Relations

Special collections, like children and rare flowers, thrive on special attention. One might even say that without a vigorous public relations program, special collections will suffer grievously. Yet once again the uniqueness of this department distinguishes it from just about every other aspect of the library: the reference department, circulation, and technical services all function without having to worry about public relations, but not so special collections. At least nine areas concern us here: exhibitions, receptions, fund-raising, social obligations, faculty relations, fellowships, publications, lectures, and, of course, the media.

### EXHIBITIONS[1]

Library exhibitions may be categorized as either major or minor. By major, I mean a large exhibit covering hundreds of square feet of area in bookcases and display tables. Filling an occasional shelf or display case with a few odds and ends would be considered minor. In this section we are talking only about major undertakings. Exhibitions are the most traditional form of public relations for special collections. Almost every special collections department has at least one exhibit a year, and the larger ones may have half a dozen or more. The purposes of an exhibition are to draw attention to your department, to display valuable items of unusual local interest, to present a series of rare works—books, manuscripts, letters, or maps—on some coordinated theme, such as nineteenth century German writers, or eighteenth century French voyagers and voyages, or the letters of Boswell. In this way an exhibition will attract new clients to the holdings, or make the library director aware of your existence, or simply reveal some of your treasures to connoisseurs and professors.

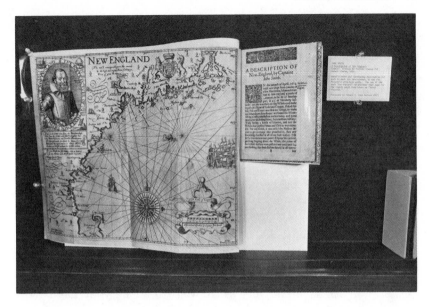

Part of exhibit at the Newberry Library, Chicago. Courtesy of the Newberry Library, Chicago

And exhibitions on loan are common. You may borrow an exhibition of Islamic works, in Persian, Arabic, and Turkish, the current vogue, or perhaps, if you have a strong American history department, you may be able to persuade Yale's curator of the Franklin Papers to lend you some choice pieces for a major display. Similarly, other libraries may ask you to provide them with exhibition materials. The curator must develop a policy about such loans and how to deal with them. Frequently, a member of the faculty or a distinguished private collector may be persuaded to place some interesting works at your disposal for an exhibition. Most professors are flattered by such requests.

If there is a major annual campus event, such as a Shakespeare festival, it is usually quite easy to get together a collection of first or second editions of that author's works. In other words, if it is possible to tie in an exhibition theme with another theme currently attracting attention on campus or in your city, take advantage of it. On the other hand, it is the curator's duty to hold exhibitions of priceless works on subjects that may be unknown even to most of the intellectual community. The curator is, after all, an educator as well. But whatever the subject, try not to crowd the articles in the display cases, prepare clean printed explanations of each item, and try to relate them all in order to maintain your theme and the public's interest.

Prepare a printed catalog for each exhibition. Usually each item on display is numbered, and then each number is explained in the published catalog, as in the following example. Let us create an exhibition entitled Emile Zola and the Dreyfus Affair, with some 250 items on display. The following actual letter (in French) is from Zola. In the catalog it would be described as follows:

151.   Autograph letter, signed, Emile Zola, to "M. Scheurer-Kestner":

"Paris, 20 November 1897

"Dear Sir,

"I have the very great wish to shake your hand most vigorously. You could not believe how your admirable attitude, so calm in the midst of threats and the most grievous harm, fills me with admiration. No matter what happens, no one could have played a greater rôle than you have, and I envy you.

"I do not know what I shall do, but I have never been so moved by any human drama. This is the fight for truth, and it is the only good one, the only great one worth fighting for. Even at the moment of apparent defeat, it is certain that victory will win out.

"With all my heartfelt best wishes,"

Zola had finally been convinced of the innocence of Captain Alfred Dreyfus, who was still on Devil's Island, and Scheurer-Kestner, an elderly and highly respected Vice President of the French Senate, had just announced publicly that he was convinced of Dreyfus's innocence. Following this letter, Zola committed himself fully to the cause of Dreyfus and began publishing a series of newspaper articles in *Le Figaro* which culminated in Zola's most famous article in January 1898, entitled "J'Accuse," which led to his own legal prosecution by the French government and his eventual flight into exile in England, but which at the same time resulted in the call for a new trial for Dreyfus as well.

Single page letter, 18 × 15 cm.
On loan from the Bibliothèque Nationale

This entry in the catalog thus provides an English translation of the French work on display and gives its significance. The citation includes the size of the letter and indicates that it is on loan from the French government. In reality, such an exhibition dedicated entirely to this theme should provide a brief historical introduction by the curator. The catalog not only helps the public understand the exhibition but also advertises your efforts. Visitors leaving the exhibit with the catalog may show it to others. Of course, the curator will want to include a copy of each catalog in the annual report.

A special collections department should mount at least four major exhibitions a year—ideally, even more— but regardless of the number, a master plan for the series of exhibitions planned for the next year or two should be drawn up so as to provide balance, continuity, and timeliness. A major exhibition may well take a few weeks to prepare, including selecting and mounting works, printing signs and catalogs, and perhaps translating certain passages, as well as writing explanations of each item's significance. Time spent on exhibitions is time that your regular staff will not be able to spend on their daily duties, and the curator must take all this into consideration.

The following is an example of seven fairly representative exhibitions mounted at Yale 1980-1981:

1. "George Eliot," celebrating the 100th anniversary of her death.
2. "Heinrich Heine and His Age: Literary Dissidence in Early Nineteenth-Century Germany."
3. "Sir Arthur Conan Doyle and Sherlock Homes."
4. "Emily Dickinson and Her World."
5. "Sterling Memorial Library: 50th Anniversary."
6. "The World of Printed Ephemera."
7. "Conservation and Preservation at Yale."

## RECEPTIONS

Receptions can fall into various categories, but chiefly they are either directly connected with an exhibition or not. Major exhibitions frequently involve at least one guest lecturer—for instance, an author speaking about his or her own works, or a professor introducing the subject at hand—followed by wine and cheese and hors d'oeuvres. Invitations to these private receptions are generally sent to specially selected guests, and they frequently take place the evening before the first public showing, or in some cases, in an afternoon, when the library is closed to the general public.

These receptions are valuable to the curator and library as a means of cultivating the interests of those who have perhaps made gifts in the past which have in turn made the exhibition possible, or who, it is hoped, will feel inclined to donate to the library if inspired by a curator who is doing a proper job. Individuals want to be remembered. There are those who may wish to establish a memorial fund on behalf of a family member or in honor of a distinguished professor, or who want to help establish an endowment fund or a bequest. Rare books only increase in value, and such an investment can be considered not only wise financially, but also one which enhances the donor's name by associating it with the great cultural works of the past.

A simple reception may be the initial step in arousing the interest of such a prospective donor. And then of course the media should be invited. It should be pointed out that because of particularly spacious facilities, wine and cheese receptions are sometimes given in the main reading room itself, but, as the curator of special collections of Stanford University told me recently, she did that once but never again, as the food attracted insects even months after the event. This is a valid consideration. Any reception involving food should preferably take place in a foyer or nearby facility, away from the books, as is done at the Hoover Institution, for instance.

Other receptions may be given to honor a distinguished guest of the university, in recognition of his or her scholarship or donations to the university. Some older libraries still maintain oak walls, marble or stone fireplaces, crystal chandeliers, and a dignified setting for such a reception. Even if the honored guest has nothing to do with special collections, it is a means of attracting attention to your holdings.

## FUND-RAISING AND SOCIAL OBLIGATIONS

Fund-raising is a major role for most curators of special collections, though large libraries also have specially appointed officers whose main task is to encourage and receive gifts and endowments. In some libraries curators are told specifically not to meddle in this field, but most curators are expected to encourage contributions to their department. Yale has gone so far as to print the forms required for such gifts, bequests, and endowments on the inside back cover of its *Bulletin of Yale University*. Individuals sometimes walk into a library and say they would like to make a donation, but in most cases the curator must go out and encourage donations. For this reason, the curator is wise to belong to certain local organizations. Take an active part in alumni affairs, belong to and contribute to the local group of bibliophiles, work on an arts council, become a member of your local historical society, join social clubs and gatherings, and tap local foundations and corporations. For other details on this subject see Chapter 8.

## FACULTY RELATIONS

As a rule, the link between special collections and the faculty is a weak one, and yet it is in the interest of the faculty and the curator to strengthen it. There are, for example, two areas that are fairly well represented in most special collections: history and literature. It behooves the curator to get to know and work with the professors in these two departments. If your collection is strong in the Italian Renaissance, for example, and a course is taught on this subject in the history department, make the professor aware of your holdings; they might be useful not only to the students, but for his or her own research as well. The same applies to literature. Indeed, the Renaissance collection may be of interest not only to your historians, but to the department of Romance languages. In such an instance, special collections could claim that its holdings were of direct use both to professors and students and specific courses taught at the university. When consulting with professors who evince a special interest in your holdings, ask them to recommend books to add to your collection and to inform you of others in the field who might wish to sell or contribute items to the library. You could even encourage meetings of these professors and some of their interested graduate students on a regular basis. The benefits of close faculty-curatorial relations are rarely cultivated, but surprisingly great.

## FELLOWSHIPS

It would be in the greatest interests of your special collections department to develop use of your collections by means of a "fellowship" program. Some wealthy patrons, interested in seeing certain pet sub-collections used, may set aside a few thousand dollars each year to be awarded to outstanding young scholars in the field. These relationships are especially important because those young scholars frequently form special attachments to your institution and not only continue to use it throughout their careers, but will encourage others to as well. The Hoover Institution has developed this to a fine art, offering a great variety of research fellowships. And of course there are grants and fellowships offered by the National Endowment for the Humanities, the American Philosophical Society, and various foundations and corporations.

## PUBLICATIONS

A small special collections department may publish only the catalogs of its special exhibitions, but the larger, well endowed library can produce catalogs, bibliographical data, monographs, microfilms, and a wide variety of materials. Every imprint bears the name of your library. The more you publish, the more seriously you are taken.

The following publications are typical examples of what a larger library might expect to put out on an annual basis. This is from *The Annual Report of the Newberry Library for the Year Ending June 30, 1982*[2]:

### NEWBERRY LIBRARY PUBLICATIONS

Cloonan, Michèle. *Preservation Priorities for Home Library Care.* 1982.

Dean, Susan, compiler. 1982 Associates' Calendar, *Lewis Carroll's Alice's Adventures in Wonderland*. 1981.

Melville, Herman. *Israel Potter*. The Writings of Herman Melville, volume 8. Edited by Harrison Hayford, Herschel Parker, and G. Thomas Tanselle. Northwestern University Press and the Newberry Library, 1982.

Spurgin, Sarah, editor. *A Newberry Newsletter*. Numbers 25-28, 1981-82.

Center for the History of the American Indian.
Bibliographical Series: The Newberry Library Center for the History of the American Indian. Francis Jennings, General Editor, Indiana University Press.
O'Donnell, James Howlet III. *Southeastern Frontiers: Europeans, Africans, and American Indians*. 1982.
Salisbury, Neal. *The Indians of New England*. 1982.
Schuster, Helen H. *The Yakimas*. 1982.
Stewart, Omer C. *Indians of the Great Basin*. 1982.
Surtees, Robert J. *Canadian Indian Policy*. 1982.
Thorton, Russell, Gary D. Sandefur, and Harold G. Grasmick. *The Urbanization of American Indians*. 1982.
Hoover, Herbert T., and David R. Miller, editors. *Meeting Ground*. Number 9, 1981.
Occasional Papers Series:
*Urban Indians*. Proceedings of the Third Annual Conference on Problems and Issues Concerning American Indians Today. Number 4, 1981.
Veeder, William H., *Indian Water Rights in the Concluding Years of the Twentieth Century*. Number 5, 1982.
Center for Renaissance Studies.
Celsi, Mino. *In Haereticis Coercendis Quatenus Progredi Liceat,* edited by G. Bietenholz. Corpus Reformatorum Italicorum, edited by Luigi Firpo, Giorgio Spini, and John A. Tedeschi. Prismi Editrice and the Newberry Library, 1982.
Herman Dunlap Smith Center for the History of Cartography.
Bosse, David, editor. *Mapline*. Numbers 24-27, 1981-82.
Revised Cartographic Slide Sets:
Claudius Ptolemy. *Geographiae Cosmographia*. Ulm, 1482.
Abraham Ortelius. *Theatrum Orbis Terrarum*. Antwerp, 1601.
Christopher Saxton. *Atlas of England*. London, 1579.
George Braun and Frans Hogenberg. *Civitates Orbis Terrarum*. Cologne, 1572-1617.
Gerard Mercator. *Atlas. Amsterdam, 1630.*

## LECTURES AND SEMINARS

If your library has the facilities, it would be useful to arrange for a regular schedule of lectures to be given in the special collections department, and these could very well attract the interested public as well. The curator may give a few lectures on his or her own field of interest or on special acquisitions, or guest lecturers could supplement these with subjects of related interest. Seminars could also be held there on occasion.

## THE MEDIA

This finally brings us to the general subject of the media. Let the press and television and radio stations know of your events; public radio and television are usually cooperative. Visiting guests and lecturers of distinction, the presentation of a new endowment fund, the opening of a new wing, the first public showing of a valuable new acquisition—all are newsworthy events. Naturally, your university newspapers and alumni bulletins would follow this up as well. The more attention focused on special collections, the more likely that your other goals will be met: an increase in gifts and donations, larger budgets, better facilities, and a larger staff.

References

1.  The following is an abbreviated bibliograpy. My first recommendation for the curator is to study examples of brochures printed for earlier exhibits at your library and at others as well, to get an idea of the variety of presentations made. After looking at those, you may wish to peruse the following.

    American Library Association. *Library/USA: A Bibliographic and Descriptive Report.* Chicago: ALA, 1967.
    This is a report on the exhibit of the U.S. at the World's Fair, 1964-65.

    Borgwardt, Stephanie. *Library Display.* 2nd ed. Johannesburg: Witwatersrand University Press, 1970.

    Bronson, Que. *Books on Display.* Washington, D.C.: Metropolitan Washington Library Council, 1982.

Coplan, Kate. *Effective Library Exhibits; How to Prepare and Promote Good Displays.* 2nd ed. Dobbs Ferry, N.Y.: Oceana Publications, 1974.

Harrison, K.C. *Public Relations for Libraries.* 2nd ed. Aldershot, Hants.: Grover Publishing Company, Ltd., 1982.

Hunter, Eric J. *Display for Librarians: A Handbook;* Written and Illustrated by Eric Hunter, With Assistance of Michael Seagroatt. 2nd ed. Liverpool: Liverpool Polytechnic, 1975.

Rummel, Kathleen Kelly, and Perica, Esther. *Persuasive Public Relations for Libraries.* Chicago: American Library Association 1983.

Usherwood, Bob. "The Visible Library," in *Practical Public Relations for Public Librarians.* London: The Library Association, 1981.

Sorrell, P. "Displaying Rare Books in the Reed Room, Dunedin Public Library," *New Zealand Libraries,* 44 (December 1983) 66-68.

2. *The Annual Report of the Newberry Library for the Year Ending June 30, 1982* (Chicago: Newberry Library, 1982, p. 16.

# 6

## Appraisals, Insurance, and Security

### APPRAISALS

Appraisals are frequently required when the library acquires gifts and bequests of books, or when insurance involves works worth more than $200 for some institutions, and over $5,000 for the Internal Revenue Service.[1] Generally libraries will recommend that a party donating a collection or substantial number of works, have them appraised, and they will provide that donor with a list of bona fide appraisers. As a rule, libraries will not make an appraisal of donated materials (for they are considered "interested parties").[2] The appraisal of the works concerned may take place at the donor's residence, or the donor may have the books shipped directly to the library and send an appraiser there to prepare a report. For reasons of liability, I should prefer to have any donated works appraised at the residence of the donor, for in the event something happened to a few thousand books sent directly to the library before appraisal, a complex situation could arise. The best appraisers cost hundreds of dollars a day plus expenses, whereas local appraisers frequently charge considerably less. It would not hurt to remind the donor that the fee for an appraisal is tax deductible.

The appraiser goes through various stages. First is the preparation of the most accurate description possible of the work at hand. The appraiser then goes through various reference works, including *Bookman's Price Index* (compiled from dealers' catalogs), *Book Auction Records,* which includes sales in several European countries commanding prices of at least £50 Sterling, and of course *American Book*

*Prices Current,* which reports any sales at American and English auctions for works worth a minimum of $50. The *Used Price Guide,* compiled by Mildred S. Mandeville, in Kenmore, Washington, is useful for current prices. Using these or other reference works, including dealers' catalogs, the appraiser attempts to establish the "fair market value" of a particular work.

When the item to be appraised is a well-known book, the problems are few, but if it is something for which no reference can be found, even going back over fifty years of auction records, then it is more difficult. Say a fairly famous philosopher wishes to sell one or more manuscripts. How does he or she know what a fair price is? It is not always easy, although the introduction of UTOPIA may at least make more up-to-date data available more quickly. UTOPIA is the computerized database begun in 1980 by *American Book Prices Current,* and though initially only going back to 1975, it daily adds about a thousand new records.[3]

But even computers cannot always help when it comes to judgment, and it is easy for the amateur to make a disastrous estimate in the value of a work. Donald Osier of the University of Minnesota provides an excellent example: In 1979 a copy of L. Frank Baum's *Wizard of Oz*—a first printing of the first edition—sold for $1,000, while another copy—also a first printing of the first edition—with some loose bindings, one missing endpaper and a water stain on the back cover fetched only $35.[4]

Rare books are generally graded according to the following four categories: "As New, or Mint Condition," meaning that it is as perfect as on the day it was published; "Fine," meaning that it looks quite new, though slightly used (with no defects); "Very Good," which means that small signs of wear are beginning to appear (but still no major defects); and "Good," in average condition.

## INSURANCE

Library insurance falls into two general categories; for the building itself and for the contents. Most libraries have a fire policy for the building itself but frequently lack a policy to cover its contents. When the contents are reduced solely to the value of the library's books, a great number of library directors are forced to admit that they have no reasonably accurate idea of what they are worth. This ignorance of the value of the library's holdings extends to the department of special collections, where the curator frequently pleads equal ignorance of the value of his or her holdings. Admittedly, it is hard, if not impossible, to give the average cost of an "average" rare book. Although a library's board of trustees is ultimately responsible for an adequate insurance program, it is up to the library director to work out the details of the policy. In addition to the two general types of policies, there are two categories of insurable risks: The first involves physical damage to property in general, and the second, losses caused by employee theft. Most all-risks policies will cover physical property insurance but rarely employee dishonesty. When employee dishonesty is not covered, it is recommended that they be bonded, either individually or by a blanket policy.

A basic fire (and lightning) policy may also be extended to cover windstorms, hail, explosions (except from boilers), riots (including strikes or civil disorders), aircraft damage, vehicle damage, and smoke damage (other than that caused by a "hostile fire"). And there are three other areas not included in such a fire policy: the nuclear exclusion (i.e., any losses resulting from nuclear or radioactive causes) the usual war risk exclusion, and a third category of special importance to libraries—water damage. This includes flood, surface water, overflow of streams, water backing up through sewers and drains, and, lastly, water below the surface of the ground surrounding the library, which seeps in and causes damage to the foundation, walls, or floors. One may also add to the regular fire policy added coverage against vandalism and malicious mischief (which generally excludes theft).[5] It should be explained that water damage resulting from a fire—turning on hoses and sprinkler systems—is covered by the fire policy, but if the sprinkler system breaks down and leaks and is not set off by a fire, then any damage it causes can only be covered by a "sprinkler leakage" policy.

Fires causing smoke and water damage have occurred at numerous university and college libraries including, for example, those at the Library of the Institute of Experimental Medicine and Surgery, the University of Montreal, the University of Florida's Law Library, the University of Hawaii, Wheaton College, Columbia University, and the University of California, Berkeley. Perhaps one of the most costly on record occurred in New York City in April 1966, at the Jewish Theological Seminary, resulting in a $3 million loss, including the loss of many rare books among the 70,000 volumes burnt, and another 150,000 which were water damaged.[6]

In 1962 the Executive Board of the American Library Association hired the Gage-Babcock organization to come up with a model insurance policy just for libraries. This policy is separate from, and assumes the existence of, a fire policy for the library building and is therefore concerned only with library contents. Obviously many of its clauses are intended for general public libraries as well, but the essential thing is that all points concentrate on library property.

The policy begins with "Perils Covered" in which it states a specific amount: "This policy in the amount of $ —— insures all risks of loss or physical damage in accordance with the terms, conditions, and limitations following."[7] Now as an "all-risks" policy this means that, unlike a standard fire policy for the building, coverage is extended to include vandalism, theft, water damage of any kind (including by flood), collapse of the building, explosion of any kind, landslide, earthquake, sand storms, damage from overheating, etc.[8] Property is protected and has very few geographical limitations, even when it is away being repaired, or on loan, or in the mail.

Under the Second Section, "Property Covered" lists the following items:

a.  On the general collections as follows:

| | | |
|---|---|---|
| Adult fiction | (a) $ | per volume |
| Adult non-fiction | (a) $ | per volume |
| Juvenile materials | (a) $ | per volume |
| Reference books | (a) $ | per volume |
| Periodicals (bound) | (a) $ | per volume |
| Periodicals (not bound) | (a) $ | per volume |
| Bound documents | (a) $ | per volume |
| Unbound documents | (a) $ | per volume |
| Newspapers before 1865 | (a) $ | per issue (per volume) |
| Newspapers 1865 to date | (a) $ | per issue (per volume) |
| Microcards (includes all forms of microprint) | (a) $ | per unit |
| Tape recordings | (a) $ | each |
| Sheet music | (a) $ | per item |
| Phonograph records | (a) $ | per record |
| Pamphlets | (a) $ | per item |
| _____ | (a) $ | per _____ |
| _____ | (a) $ | per _____ |

b. On administrative and holdings records:

| | | |
|---|---|---|
| Shelf list | (a) $ | per card |
| Adult catalog | (a) $ | per card |
| Juvenile catalog | (a) $ | per card |
| Registration cards | (a) $ | per card |
| Withdrawal records | (a) $ | per card |
| Microfilm | (a) $ | per reel |
| _____ | (a) $ | per _____ |
| _____ | (a) $ | per _____ |

c. On manuscripts, rare books, and special collection materials:

  _____  (a) $
  _____  (a) $
  _____  (a) $
  _____  (a) $

d. On individually described pictures, paintings, sculpture, or other fine arts:

  _____  (a) $
  _____  (a) $
  _____  (a) $
  _____  (a) $

e. And on similar property of the Insured, not specifically scheduled, but limited to an amount not to exceed 10 percent of the policy amount and then not for more than $250 on any one item:

f. And on furniture, fixtures, tools, equipment, supplies, and similar property owned by the Insured Library or in its care or custody, and improvements and betterments to buildings not owned by the Insured Library, and subject to a limit of $250, the personal property of any one officer or employee:[9]

This general policy on contents obviously requires higher sums today, and other categories, involving more recently developed equipment, such as computer tapes and equipment, microfiches, etc., but in essence it represents what was needed. What is noteworthy for the curator is that two categories have been included which heretofore had only been issued as separate policies: Valuable Papers and Fine Arts. Roland Baughman, Head of Special Collections at Columbia, endorsed this type of policy when it first appeared.[10]

 Three separate policies should, nevertheless, be discussed: Fine Arts, Valuable Papers, and Transit Insurance. As the items in special collections can be considered in either the Fine Arts or the Valuable Papers Policies, both are to be considered, since valuable papers are not covered adequately in the standard fire policy.

## The Fine Arts Policy

As a rule, fine arts include paintings, etchings, tapestries, pictures "and other bona fide works of art." This is an all-risks policy but each article is appraised and written down with a separate value, item by item. It states that a limited sort of "blanket insurance may be written on any other property of this type not to exceed 10 percent of the insurance on scheduled items. Recovery on articles under the blanket item will be on an actual cash value basis and subject to a 100 percent coinsurance provision."

Property under the Fine Arts policy is subject to the usual exclusions of war risks, nuclear energy, wear and tear, gradual deteriorations, moths, vermin, inherent vice, and damage from any repairing, restoring or retouching process.

## The Valuable Papers and Rare Books Policy

This policy was established to cover all valuable books and records, whether printed or written, and does so on an all-risks basis.

The property insured under a Valuable Papers Policy may be either scheduled on an agreed-amount basis or may be covered in a blanket item on an actual cash-value basis. If property cannot be replaced, it must be scheduled on the agreed-amount basis and cannot be included in the blanket item.

The exclusions under this policy are wear and tear, gradual deterioration, vermin and inherent vice, war risks, nuclear damage, dishonesty of any insured partner, officer, director, or trustee, and (unless caused by lightning), electrical or magnetic injury or erasure of electronic recordings.

It will be noted that employee dishonesty is not excluded except as indicated above. In the case of libraries there is an exclusion of loss from failure of borrowers to return books or valuable papers.

This policy is very useful for insuring all books, papers, and records in a library, particularly the large values represented in card catalog systems.

It is important to be sure that property specifically insured under a Fine Arts policy or Valuable Papers policy is excluded from the general contents coverage.

This policy provides that 10 percent of the total amount of the insurance is extended to cover property while being conveyed outside the premises or while temporarily at other premises, exept for storage.[12]

## Transit Insurance

Transit insurance may be required by your library. The other policies mentioned above are limited in their transit coverage in that fairs or expositions are not always coverd. When materials go to an outside bindery, it must be established who assumes liability should anything untoward occur.

Water damage insurance is another consideration. The 1982 water-main disaster at Yale is a vivid reminder not to neglect this item. To quote the ALA's *Protecting the Library and Its Resources,*

> ... the protection available under the Fine Arts and Valuable Papers policies would include water damage and should be a better method of protecting books and similar property than the alternative of carrying this coverage under a separate water damage policy.[13]

Interestingly enough, many insurance companies claim they have no standard valuable papers policy. Each policy is so dependent upon the unique qualities of a particular rare books collection and its physical surroundings (including security systems and fire prevention devices) that most companies will not even supply an estimate for this service, but those libraries that have applied for it have found it very expensive. One must consider the cost of such a policy over a period of years and the actual value of the collection. Is it worth the added cost of appraisals? Most university libraries with an "average" special collections department carry no special coverage for valuable books and papers. On the other hand, a library that spends in the range of six or seven digits annually to acquire and preserve books needs a valuable papers policy at least for major items. But even if smaller or medium-sized libraries and collections elect not to take out the valuable papers policy, they must weigh other possibilities, including a water damage policy.

The policy that may prove the best compromise for most university collections is a "blanket property policy," combined with "all-risks" as a part of a basic fire policy. This one policy covers every building and all their contents. This all-risks blanket property policy would take building by building, and put a value on each, based on the physical structure and its contents. It would not go into nearly as much detail on contents as the policy recommended by the ALA nor even of a valuable papers and records policy (i.e., individual titles of books are not listed). Let us say, for example, that there are seven libraries on campus, and the special collections department is one which I will call the Smith Library. Under the blanket property policy, there would only be half a dozen items listed under "The Smith Library," e.g.,

Regular books: no. of volumes × rates = insured value
Rare books: no. of volumes × rate = insured value
Manuscripts: no. of pages × rate = insured value

In one 1983 insurance report I read, the average price for a new book was set at $25.48 plus cataloging cost of $15 per volume, or a total of $40.48 per volume. After bringing in several experts from their company, the insuring firm established the average value per rare book at $77.77 which was multiplied by the number of volumes in the special collections department. If the Smith Library's special collections department had 100,000 volumes, the rare books would be insured for $7,777,000. If this university held a blanket property policy worth $900,000,000, less a deductible amount of $100,000, and all the rare books holdings were destroyed, the library would collect $7,777,000 less the first $100,000 or a total of $7,677,000. Following the destruction of that collection, of course, the curator would be required to provide a copy of the card catalog and that, one hopes will have been microfilmed and stored elsewhere.

Given the high rate of insuring rare books under the valuable papers policy, this blanket property policy seems far less expensive and therefore more realistic, for it also covers all types of water damage, employee theft, etc., though it retains the usual special exclusions listed under both the fine arts policy and the valuable papers policy regarding war, nuclear damage, vermin, etc. Despite the high rates for the valuable papers policy, its advantage over the blanket property policy is that it does not have a high deductible amount. If, for instance, in the example discussed above with the fire in the special collections department of the Smith Library, the damage had only come to $100,000, the insurance company would have paid none of it. Most insurance groups would probably provide the all-risks, blanket property policy discussed above and the Kemper Group definitely does. Everything is negotiable and dependent upon such things as your library's own fire record and the sort of security system you have. The problem of theft by non-employees still must be covered by a separate policy, however, and is known as a "comprehensive crime policy." The curator and library director or the agent representing the library and university must keep in mind that the amounts set in blanket property policy for rare books and manuscripts must be carefully analyzed and "an agreed amount" established in writing. Any agreement with your insurance agent must be in writing.

A variety of policies are available to libraries containing special collections: fire policies, the special ALA library policy, a fine arts policy, a valuable papers and records policy, and a blanket property, all-risks fire policy. There is obviously no single policy which can be recommended universally, and every curator and library director must decide which one best fits their needs.

## SECURITY AND THE EMERGENCY PLAN

Because most libraries and related institutions do not have the majority of their works appraised and insured for a specific value, the question of security and care of the department's valuable works assumes even greater significance. Certain elementary steps can be taken to minimize the possibilities of harm coming to the library's holdings, for instance, by using fireproof materials in the building, furnishings, and equipment, by installing smoke detectors, chemical sprays, and by building a large fireproof vault for the rarest and most precious items in a collection.[14] But here "security" provides a different set of problems, especially for rare items, for the number and variety of electronic devices frequently used in the regular stacks and which can be used is greatly reduced, as the curator naturally wishes to tamper as little as possible with a rare item. The general rule is not to apply sensing devices of any kind to rare items. Nevertheless, there are certain basic steps that provide greater protection for rare materials.

### Records and Identification of Materials

It is recommended by the Society of American Archivists to take a complete inventory of special collections at least once every three years, for without a complete list of holdings, how is one to know that nothing is missing? This naturally is a tedious task when it means getting out the Hollinger boxes and enumerating every item, though this frequently is not done by the curator. There is nothing easier for a thief than to steal one famous letter out of a box containing fifty—how often are these items counted?

One of the problems with monitoring stolen items from a special collection is that they are rarely marked as library property. Books and manuscripts can be marked in a variety of ways, including bookplates, embossing, perforation, invisible ink, indelible ink, or 3M's new "microtaggant" invisible markings. In circulating libraries, a variety of electronic devices are employed because students have direct access to stacks, and because these materials are checked out as part of the circulating collection. Although some special collections do allow limited direct access to materials, most do not, and materials are never checked out or circulated except as interlibrary loans.

Marking books with the library's stamp is another concern. Some curators do not approve of bookplates, others do not like any type of embossing, or perforating, and most disapprove of invisible markings. Alice Harrison Bahr, in her useful work *Book Theft and Library Security Systems, 1981-1982,*[15] discusses a new type of ink developed by the Library of Congress for marking books and manuscripts. It is indelible and does not blot or fade. The Library of Congress's assistant director of preservation will send a small free sample to libraries. But, of course, some curators will allow only pencil to be used for writing call numbers on the inside cover or the first leaf of a rare book (along with accession information on the back leaf or cover), for fear of reducing the value of the original work, though others argue for the use of permanent ink for recording the name of the library and presumably the accession number.[16] Feelings are very strong on this issue.

Indeed, a specific, permanent mark designating your library must be placed on each item for security purposes. As president of the Antiquarian Booksellers Association of America, John Jenkins recommended specific locations for the library's identification device in books and manuscripts:

1. *Medieval and Renaissance Manuscripts*
   On the verso of the first leaf of the principal text, on the inner margin, approximate to the last line of text.
2. *Incunabula and Early Printed Books*
   Same as for number one.
3. *Leaf Books, Single Leaves from Manuscripts, etc.*
   On either verso or recto, at the lower portion of the text or image of

each leaf. (If an illustration of special importance is on one side, place the mark on the other.)

4. *Broadsides, Prints, Maps, Single Leaf Letters, Documents*
   On the verso, in the lower margin of the area occupied by text or image on the opposite side.

5. *Multiple Leaf Manuscript Letters, Documents, Newspapers, Ephemera*
   On the verso of the first leaf in the lower margin. An additional mark may be added on a later page where a valuable, famous signature may appear.

6. *Modern Printed Books, Pamphlets, Serial Issues*
   On the verso of the first leaf of the opening text directly below the final line. Spare the title page, half-title, and dedicatory pages.

7. *Kind of Ink and Equipment*
   Use a permanent ink that can be applied in minute quantities. The ink and equipment (rubber stamp and balsa wood pad) are described in the Library of Congress's Preservation Leaflet No. 4, *Marking Manuscripts*.

8. *Form and Size of Mark*
   Keep to a minimum size (e.g., five-point lettering). The form should be made up of initials identifying the institution as succinctly as possible, based on the National Union Catalog symbols, and suitable for arranging in lists to circulate to dealers, auction houses, collectors, etc.[17]

In 1972, the Rare Books Group of the British Library Association and the Antiquarian Booksellers' Association met to discuss the disturbing and growing problem of book and manuscript theft,[18] and they decided to publish a list of stolen rare materials. In this country, this is done by the Society of American Archivists under the title *National Register of Lost or Stolen Archival Materials,* a much-needed and welcome service. This list includes only those books or manuscripts that have been missing for less than twenty years and have unique distinguishing marks of identification. Microfilm, artifacts, maps, and related items can also be registered if they are one of a kind.[19] The *National Register* is a bimonthly publication which also includes other information—the names of dealers and collectors known to deal in stolen books, manuscripts, and related materials. The Society of American Archivists does not charge for the report of a missing item. For other items which may be rare and valuable but which do not meet the criteria established by the *National Register, AB Bookman's Weekly* lists books reported missing from shops and libraries.[20] Alice Bahr also recommends two other publications concerning archival security: Timothy Walch's *Archives and Manuscripts: Security,* published by the Society of American Archivists, and the *Archival Security Newsletter,* covering everything from theft to new security systems.[21] The SAA's security consulting service may also be called upon by your library when designing or studying facilities.

Other measures can be taken in the case of stolen or missing rare books, such as use of the computer, as J.L. Chernofsky reminds us,[22] and of course there are other organizations to be contacted as well. A computer system known by the unfortunate acronym BAM-BAM (Bookline Alert—Missing Books and Manuscripts) is now in effect, to retain details of all stolen and missing books and manuscripts. When completed, this system will have interlibrary connections throughout North America and Europe. Full information about stolen or missing articles from your library should be sent to any or all of the following. If the materials have a value of less than $5,000, do not contact either John Jenkins or the FBI, but if they exceed $5,000 in value, or if a theft includes a number of items worth more than $100 each, then contact both Jenkins and the FBI.[23]

Antiquarian Booksellers Association of America
National Headquarters
50 Rockefeller Plaza
New York, NY 10020

BAM-BAM
*American Book Prices Current*
121 East 78th Street
New York, NY 10021

Dr. Terry Belanger
Assistant Dean, School of Library Service
Columbia University
New York, NY 10027
(212) 280-2292

Mr. John H. Jenkins
Security Chairman
Antiquarian Booksellers Association
Austin, TX
(512) 444-6616 or at night (512) 478-8164

Agent James McShane
U.S. Customs
New York, NY
(212) 466-5506
(If it is feared that the stolen items might be sent abroad.)

Agent Mike Burns
Federal Bureau of Investigation
Austin, TX
(512) 478-8501

Concern about the increasing number of thefts of rare books and manuscripts was acknowledged at the American Library Association's 1982 convention in Philadelphia,[24] though of course this sort of crime dates back to the first tomb robbers of ancient Egypt. Today special collections curators must face reality and decide on specific measures for permanently marking their properties, despite the arguments of "purists" to whom such tampering is nothing short of desecration. Descriptive bibliographical data, while sometimes available, especially in the field of incunabula, does not have nearly the same impact on the police and authorities as a bookplate or stamp bearing the name of your library, which provide immediate identification. A book or manuscript should be plated, stamped with a catalog number, and preferably bearing an accession number as well.

This information must be recovered by the librarian in his or her records, along with a full bibliographical description, and even photographs and microfilm if possible. And after all, if there are not proper shelf and catalog records, who is to know what is missing? The records should include the accession number, which is recorded in your Accession Register, or the modern equivalent, which immediately establishes all information regarding provenance, including date acquired, the price, and the shop or person acquired from. If all these records are not kept up to date, even regular inventories are useless. I like a good set of photographs of the spine, covers, and at least the title page and frontispiece. A photograph can be easily reproduced and sent to the authorities should materials disappear, although a good critical bibliographical description would reveal much more detail.

Once an item is inventoried, all the pertinent data should be recorded on that inventory card to indicate that each work was duly checked, when, by whom, and its condition at the time of each inspection (see Figure 1). If the condition of the book has changed drastically

FIGURE 1   Inventory Card

Author: _____ Call No: _____

Short-title and number of volumes: _____

Place of Publication: _____

Year Published: _____ Edition: _____

Accession Number: _____

Special Information: _____

Original Cover: (vellum, cloth, quarter-calf, etc.) _____

_____

Condition of Book
v. good, average, poor

Inventory by _____

Date of Inventory _____

since the last inventory, the files must be checked to see who has used it
since then, or if an "inhouse" accident has occurred (librarians have
been known to drop books accidentally from ladders and desk tops!).

## Monitoring and Surveillance

It is distasteful to librarians to have to "spy" on scholars and
visitors using their facilities, and it is usually impossible to assure complete surveillance despite the presence of a librarian or clerk in a room
with patrons using the collection. Even when television monitors are
employed, as at the Hunt Institute, there is rarely someone watching
non-stop. There are other considerations as well.

You must, for example, be able to trust your own staff. Were they
all thoroughly checked out before being hired? University faculty frequently have to be cleared by an FBI authorization before being hired,
but not so non-professional library staff. Not long ago, a clerk at a circulation desk in the Los Angeles Public Library was caught red-handed
and imprisoned.[25] Library personnel or the curator must check references carefully, and this includes student help.

The visitor to special collections must receive the curator's authorization to use the collection, although many university special collections do this in a fairly slipshod manner. Anyone using a special collection must provide adequate proof of purpose and personal identification showing a photograph. In short, the visitor must be a bona fide scholar, or special visitor, working on bona fide research. Remember the ex-student who was caught stealing at Princeton University not so long ago.[26] All briefcases and bags must be checked at the point of entry, preferably outside the reading room. You may even require that briefcases and bags be opened at the point of departure. There are rare book collections in this country where there is no attempt to make the visitor check in all books and briefcases at the desk, nor any attempt to inspect them when the visitor leaves, though one hopes such libraries are few and far between. At the Archives of the Hoover Institution, a rigorous procedure is followed, and all briefcases and bags are checked into lockers. Most libraries not using electronic surveillance systems have a guard inspecting all materials leaving the library. At the special collections department of the Green Library at Stanford, one cannot enter the main reading room without first receiving permission from a desk attendant who requires identification, and the completion of cards for the books requested. As a student in England many years ago, I found library officials to be quite lax on security. Several years later I was doing research on Lord Salisbury and Fashoda, I had to study the Marquis's papers at Christ Church College, Oxford. I introduced myself to the keeper of books there and explained that I was an American college professor doing research on the British Prime Minister. He welcomed me to the archive but refused to take any form of identification from me. Anyone at Christ Church obviously was to be taken at his or her word. This was the British attitude for a good many years, although a guard now goes through briefcases of those leaving the Bodleian, and photographic identification is now mandatory there.

To gain access to the Bibliothèque Nationale or the Archives Nationales, Paris, the visitor must be armed with a letter of introduction from his or her institution, sealed then with the blessing of the U.S. Cultural Attaché in the Paris embassy, or he or she may simply obtain a letter of introduction from the French Cultural Attaché in New York.

Control of the visiting scholar on the premises is a problem, given recent losses by libraries. It is not unusual for the visitor to be placed at a table with perhaps a librarian or staff member sitting somewhere in the room, and at the same time to have staff coming in occasionally with trucks of books to be shelved. Meanwhile the reader completes the call slips, hands them to the librarian, and then waits for the materials; the reader is almost never given direct access to the stacks. Sometimes the trucks are left standing unattended in the main reading room, and sometimes there are books on shelves, accessible to anyone. I have frequently browsed through books left by the staff in the reading room. But if briefcases are not checked in before entering the room, books could quickly and quietly disappear when the librarian is otherwise occupied, for there are rarely more than two or three persons in a reading room at any one time. Perhaps the best approach to the problem is to have the reader check in a briefcase and other paraphernalia in an outer room and then enter a glass-enclosed room containing only tables and chairs, as is the procedure at the Beinecke. The furniture is very modern and comfortable, although one does feel that one is sitting in a fishbowl, as the reader is observable even from outside the spacious

Reading room of the Beinecke Rare Book and Manuscript Library. Yale University. Courtesy of Ezra Stoller Associates

reading room. No carts of books pass through the Beinecke's reading room.

## Book Theft

Some pretty curious things have happened to books and manuscripts throughout the ages—they have been burned, buried, and destroyed—but the most common menace to rare book libraries today is still the one that has worried librarians throughout the centuries: bibliokleptomania. Book theft has occurred in a variety of guises, often by most distinguished perpetrators. One of the nastiest deeds committed is by the thief who "extracts," i.e., cuts or tears out certain parts of books or manuscripts. Today this is quite a common problem with science periodicals, but one of the costliest and most colorful incidents involved one Rapisardi who was caught by the Italian police after cutting out forty-one miniatures from an eleventh-century manuscript in the Vatican Library.[27] Needless to say, Vatican security has since been tightened as a result.

But the theft of entire books has traditionally been the biggest problem, whether we are dealing with one or two select works or entire libraries. Some of the first Roman libraries were stolen from the Greeks by conquering Roman generals, and large-scale plundering of libraries by invading armies has continued into this century. And yet there is something almost comforting in the knowledge that crooked generals and politicians have sought books as a primary form of loot. It may even be argued that when Mithridates of Pontus was defeated by the forces of the Roman Republic, and his large library transported to the estate of M. Licinius Lucullus in Tuscany, the manuscripts were not only safeguarded, but also made available to scholars. Indeed, so highly regarded was scholarship in classical times that we find Cicero complaining that his most trusted slave had stolen some valuable manuscripts.[28] Theft of books and manuscripts from monastic libraries during the Middle Ages by members (of all ranks) of the clergy was considered commonplace, hence the chaining of books. Lawrence S. Thompson ranks biblioklepts in the following order: "Close on the heels of the librarian comes the clergyman, and the scholar. As a big operator, the professional thief ranks considerably behind the librarian and the clergyman."[29]

The fact remains that the array of bibliokleptomania is both impressive and curious, including among the ranks of the guilty aristocrats as well as high state officials. They have included the wealthy English "collector" Sir Edward Fitzgerald, who after fleeing Britain with a list of select thefts to his credit ended up in a French prison, and the celebrated Florentine nobleman, Count Libri Carrucci della Sommaia, who was professor of mathematics at the Collège de France and Secretary to a royal commission (appointed to make an inventory of manuscripts in French public libraries), when he began "collecting" in earnest, netting a fortune at book auctions in England where he had his booty transferred, and finally ended in his conviction by a French court resulting in a sentence of ten years and the erasure of his name as a Chevalier of the Legion of Honor. Thompson was right, of course, when he suggested that a large number of librarians proved to be skillful thieves. Alois Pichler, a Bavarian scholar, was nabbed by the Russian authorities in the nineteenth century after stealing over four thousand volumes from the Imperial Public Library in St. Petersburg and ended up in a Siberian prison; another librarian, Joseph Urdich, of the University of Graz Library, stole several thousand volumes over a period of many years, but successfully falsified library records to cover his tracks.[30] Yet another German, Johann Georg Tinius, was a rabid bibliophile, and finding it impossible to acquire on a clergyman's stipend the works he desired, ultimately committed at least two murders to satisfy his unquenchable bibliomania, enabling him to accumulate a private library of nearly sixty thousand volumes before he was finally arrested, tried, convicted, and sentenced to twelve years at hard labor.[31]

The United States has not been without its notable biblioklepts, especially during the Depression in the 1930s when Joseph Francis de Vallieres d'Or stole five hundred valuable works from the Washington, D.C., residence of General David L. Brainard, whose house he was leasing. And Harold B. Clark, when tracked down by police, was found to be in the possession of hundreds of works missing from the Harvard College Library. Age was apparently no deterrent to eighty-four year old Milton Miller, who managed to steal dozens of tomes from his alma mater, the University of Pennsylvania.[32] The list goes on.

More recently, Andrew P. Antippas, a professor visiting the Yale libraries, was convicted in 1979 of stealing five valuable maps and spent a year in prison.[33] The losses suffered by libraries are sometimes amazing. The University of California at Davis discovered that forty-two volumes of *Curtis's Botanical Magazine* and another sixteen volumes of *Paxton's Magazine of Botany* had been stolen.[34] But even paintings and Chinese vases have been stolen from special collections.[35] If these works had been in the Beinecke's glass-enclosed reading room, such thefts probably could not have happened. How the Felix Frankfurter diaries were stolen from the manuscripts division of the Library of Congress still remains a mystery,[36] as does the loss of nine folders taken from the Attorney General's files stored in the National Archives, and a similar theft from the Archives of Ontario, Canada.[37] This all simply bears out the unpleasant reality that no one seems immune to theft. The most notorious recent case involved rare books stolen by one James Shinn, who was captured by the FBI only after successfully looting several libraries, and though the FBI located $250,000 worth of rare books in Shinn's Bethelehem, Pennsylvania, warehouse, they estimate that he took at least $500,000 worth of books! As for Shinn, he was sentenced to twenty years in prison.[38] Theft is becoming so common that nearly two dozen articles appear in library journals annually on this subject.

Physical access to most special collections is generally limited to one or two unlocked doors at most, with attendants at the entrance. Local fire regulations may require that additional exits be available as well, though the latter at least can be equipped with alarm systems. Janitors must never be allowed to enter a special collections department before or after hours. This is a simple precaution, but it can save a lot of anxiety.

Regardless of the type of surveillance established, however, the emphasis on security has, regrettably, changed the atmosphere in libraries and special collections throughout the country. I personally dislike having a guard go through my briefcase or, at work over a rare book, looking up to see a television camera following my every movement. A certain spirit, a very special quality, formerly taken for granted in special collections, has suffered because of the precautions we have been forced to take, and yet we have had no choice.

## The Emergency Plan

Every library department must be prepared for emergencies, and two types are of special concern to the curator of special collections: fire and flooding or water damage. The emergency plan for special collections must be written and available in an emergency. The telephone number of the nearest fire department and the closest fire alarm in the building must be known. The emergency plan should indicate where endangered manuscripts and books (according to their importance and value) should be brought. If a fireproof vault exists, for instance, the materials should be taken there. If there are emergency chemical dispensers, all librarians should be trained in their use, just as all personnel should be informed that they are not to use water. In the event of fire and the lack of a fireproof vault, a temporary secure area in the library should be designated for special collections materials, and another area should be established in another building, should the entire library building be threatened. Facilities in other buildings should be arranged ahead of time and indicated in the emergency plan.

The second part of the emergency plan, and one which seems to be called for too frequently, involves water damage resulting from the use of hoses during a fire, from flooding, broken pipes, or antiquated sprinkler systems. Again, everything must be written out—who is to do what at each stage? Into what containers are the materials to be placed, and where are these book containers located? In the event of flooding, emergency trucks must be assigned to take the damaged books and manuscripts to a cold storage facility near the library. Obviously the library director should have made these arrangements ahead of time. Once the books reach the cold storage facility, a second phase of the plan would go into effect, for an expert in treating water-damaged materials, an individual who had been designated when the emergency plan was drafted, would take charge of treating the materials. Again it must be stressed that a written emergency plan must be prepared well in advance, and the key staff members must know their roles in it.

## References

1. See Chapter 7 for the specific application of appraisals to gifts.
2. Donald V. Osier, "Appraising Library Material Donation, An Explanation of the Appraisal Process for Librarians," *Minnesota Libraries,* 26, No. 3 (August 1979), 479–83. Osier feels that a librarian who is called in to make an appraisal should use a personal letterhead, not the library's, and current tax legislation reinforces that view.
3. William Z. Schenck, "Evaluating and Valuing Gift Materials," *Library Acquisitions: Practice and Theory,* 6, No. 1 (1982), 33–40.
4. Osier, p. 479.
5. *Protecting the Library and Its Resources, A Guide to Physical Protection and Insurance. Report on a Study Conducted by Gage-Babcock & Associates, Inc.* (Chicago: American Library Association, 1963), LTP Publications No. 7 pp. 121, 140.

6. *Ibid.*, pp. 228–30. See also *Protection of Library Collections* (Boston: National Fire Protection Association, 1970), pp. 4–5. This is sometimes referred to as NFPA No. 10.

7. *Protecting the Library and Its Resources.* Chapter 14 explains the model policy paragraph by paragraph.

8. *Ibid.*

9. *Ibid.*, Reprinted by permission of the American Library Association.

10. *Ibid.*, pp. 265–68.

11. *Ibid.*

12. *Ibid.*, p. 142.

13. *Ibid.*, p. 140.

14. This vault or one elsewhere on the campus, or at a bank, should contain a microfilm of your entire card catalog in the event of fire or other disaster. (As most libraries are replacing the card catalog with microfiches, that job is saved, but there remains the shelflist.)

15. Alice Harrison Bahr, *Book Theft and Library Security Systems, 1981–1982* (White Plains, N.Y.: Knowledge Industry Publications, 1981).

16. John H. Jenkins, *Rare Books and Manuscript Thefts. A Security System for Librarians, Booksellers and Collectors* (New York: Antiquarian Booksellers Association of America, 1982). p. 24. Roderick Cave agrees on this point, *Rare Book Librarianship* (2nd revised ed., London: Clive Bingley, 1982), 66–67.

17. Jenkins.

18. Bahr, p. 116. See also, "National Register of Lost or Stolen Archival Materials," *Library and Archival Security,* 3 (Fall-Winter 1980), 63–96.

19. To register missing works, write the Society of American Archivists, Archival Security Program, Box 8198, University of Illinois, Chicago Circle, Chicago, IL 60680.

20. *A B Bookman's Weekly,* Box BW, Clifton, NJ 07015.

21. Bahr, p. 116.

22. J.L. Chernofsky, "Computerized System to Alert Trade to Thefts," *A B Bookman's Weekly,* 67 (June 29, 1981), 5058.

23. Jenkins, p. 14.

24. M. Sanders, "Joint Program on Theft in Libraries," *Library of Congress Information Bulletin,* 41 (Oct. 22, 1982), 346–48.

25. "LAPL Circulation Clerk Nailed for Theft," *Library Journal,* 107 (Sept. 1, 1982), 1580.

26. "Princeton Catches a Thief; Ex-Student Faces Trial," *Library Journal,* 107 (April 15, 1982), 767.

27. Lawrence S. Thompson, "Notes on Bibliokleptomania," in William Targ's *Carrousel for Bibliophiles, A Treasury of Tales, Narratives, Songs, Epigrams and Sundry Studies Relating to a Noble Theme* (New York: Philip C. Duchenes, 1947) p. 101.

28. *Ibid.*, pp. 101–103.
29. *Ibid.*, p 109.
30. *Ibid.*, p. 115.
31. *Ibid.*, p. 126.
32. *Ibid.*, p. 136.
33. "Yale and Newberry Recover Stolen Maps," *American Libraries* 10, No. 3 (March 1979), 100.
34. "Mail Box," *AB Bookman's Weekly* (Dec. 6, 1971), 1756.
35. "Art Works Stolen from Two New England Libraries," *Library Journal* 100, No. 13 (Sept. 15, 1975), 1592.
36. Philip P. Mason, "Archival Security. New Solutions to an Old Problem," *The American Archivist*, 38, No. 4 (Oct. 1975), 480, 484.
37. D. Russell, "Theft of Letters from the Archives of Ontario," *Library and Archival Security*, 3 (Fall-Winter 1980), 43–62.
38. "Shinn Cache of Stolen Books Uncovered in Pennsylvania," *Library Journal*, 107 (Feb. 15, 1982), 386; and "Shinn Gets Twenty Years for Stealing Rare Books," *American Libraries*, 13, (Nov. 1982), 612.

# 7

# Gifts, Exchanges, and Endowments

Unlike other library departments, most special collections depend essentially on gifts of books and manuscripts to build their holdings. Such donations are made for many reasons—philanthropic, for tax purposes, because of a special interest of the donor in the development of a certain subject area, or perhaps simply because the donor has inherited a collection and has no interest in keeping it. But if gifts make the development of special collections possible, and indeed are the very backbone of the library, they can also be a source of considerable anxiety to the curator if certain procedures are not followed carefully. In addition to donations, and regular purchases, special collections occasionally receive books through exchanges with other libraries and institutions (though this is rare), or through purchases made possible by endowment funds.

## THE GIFTS POLICY AND CRITERIA

The process of defining the collection's priorities, as discussed in Chapter One, must be applied once more when books are offered to the special collections department, for they must be vetted, to see whether or not they fall within the prescribed subject areas and meet other requirements such as chronological limits, language categories, etc. Frequently only a portion of the books offered do meet the criteria established in the acquisition policy—which means, of course, that the policy is doing precisely what it was designed to do—but they might be important enough acquisitions to warrant accepting the whole collection. And yet, as a rule, the virtual inundation of materials offered to some libraries makes the strict adherence to the acquisition policy necessary.

Most large libraries have a special Gifts and Exchange Office charged with the task of accepting or rejecting donations on behalf of the institution. In the case of special collections, however, the final responsibility for judging the worthiness of the books offered rests with the curator, whose knowledge is so specialized that few other librarians would be considered competent to make such an evaluation, though a subject specialist from a university might be consulted as well. Nor must one forget that part of the curator's concern is the physical condition of the materials. Are the leather bindings rotting? Do the pages have water or acidity damage? Are there missing plates? How much time and money would have to be spent to restore the collection, if that is even possible? This could also be a lengthy procedure, for the curator would then have to consult the marketplace and the holdings of other libraries to establish whether or not the works in question are held elsewhere or if it might not be cheaper in the long run for the library to obtain them separately. It is possible that the curator could decide to decline the proposed collection for these reasons alone, irrespective of subject suitability.

Should the collection in question pass muster, physically, and meet the requirements of the acquisition policy, the curator now refers to special policy guidelines on the subject of gifts. If a portion, perhaps even a large portion, of this collection does not meet the criteria described in the guidelines, he or she must decide on its disposition. If, for instance, only forty percent of the books offered are appropriate to the collection, and another forty percent would be of use in the general stacks of the library, while the remaining twenty percent are of no use whatsoever, how free is the curator to act?[1] The document of acceptance of a donated collection will determine how much latitude the library has in disposing of it. Policies must be drawn up not only to provide consistent guidelines for the curator and his or her staff, but for donors as well. A general policy statement should be presented to the prospective donor, in order to avoid any possible misunderstandings. Columbia University's gift acceptance policy provides an excellent example:

> It is the policy of the Libraries that gifts of materials be accepted with the understanding that upon receipt they are owned by the University and become part of the Libraries and that, therefore, the library administration

reserves the right to determine their retention, location, cataloguing treatment, and other considerations related to their use or disposition.

Books, manuscripts, and archival material[2] may be given to libraries in one of five ways: orally, or by letter, will, deed, or deposit agreement.[3] Sometimes an individual walks into a library or historical society and hands the librarian some old papers or books without even asking for a receipt. More common is the transfer of ownership through an exchange of letters; the donor states his or her desire to give the library certain items, and the library then accepts the offer in writing. The use of the donor's will as the conveying instrument is even more common,[4] as is a simple deed of gift. A deed is defined as a written instrument conveying some legal disposition of property and which must be signed by both the donor and the library, then sealed and delivered by the donor to indicate contractual offer and acceptance. The fifth means is by a document referred to as a deposit agreement, which deposits certain materials (on loan) in the library for safekeeping and contains a statement of intent to transfer title of that property, usually at an indefinite point in the future. Trudy Peterson recommends that the deposit agreement also state the library's liability for any accidental damage, as well as whatever types of cataloging and archival preservation work are expected. Regardless of the means used to convey title, all legal documents should specify what disposition the library can make of its new property, e.g., granting the library the right to transfer or sell some or all of the material.

What happens when the library is not given carte blanche in the disposition of a collection? Frequently, donors ask that the collection they are offering be set aside in a special room and be named for them, or at the very least, that the collection be accepted in toto and not be broken up. Such requests are common enough. Or a donor may stipulate that only certain qualified scholars have access to the collection, or that the names of researchers be submitted to the donor for approval, or that whatever is quoted from the collection for publication first receive the donor's approval—though requests of this nature are somewhat unusual. The donor could also give responsibility to the librarian to decide who may have access to restricted materials. There is also the matter of restricted material that is not to be shown. Barbara Kaiser feels that "restricting all letters in a collection to or about living persons is unrealistic in terms of demands made upon a library staff" and that consequently either only a part of the "restricted" collection should be made available for limited use, or that the entire collection should be withdrawn.[5]

In most cases, fortunately, the donor releases the collection totally and unconditionally, though libraries frequently agree to naming this new collection after the donor. So adamant are most libraries about accepting collections without restrictions of any kind, for fear of finding themselves "saddled with an intolerable burden" in future years, that most donors know ahead of time what to expect.[6]

During negotiations for the tentative transfer of a collection to a library, the library's representative should keep two other possibilities in mind. First, could a "continuing relationship" be established with the prospective donor through an agreement that he or she will continue to donate books or manuscripts in installments over the next several years?[7] This could all be stated in the original document. Second, the library should inquire whether or not the donor could either contribute an initial lump sum to help meet the cost of accessioning and cataloging (and perhaps binding), or, better yet, provide an endowment fund for its maintenance and future development. It cannot be stressed enough that the curator must never accept donated collections without first considering the full budgetary effects over the next decade or so.

When considering the acceptance of a collection, the curator should consider the following criteria:

1. Does the proposed collection fall within the collecting priorities stated in the acquisition policy, and would this donation not only fulfill a subject requirement, but enrich the collection as well?
2. Even if the collection under consideration does not meet the priorities stated in the acquisition policy, and indeed covers a totally different subject field, might it nevertheless be of such unusual value as to warrant acceptance (if funded properly)?
3. Could this material be obtained on loan from another library, say for an exhibition?
4. Is there, or will there be, enough space in the library to accomodate this collection properly?
5. Has sufficient funding been provided—either from the budget or the donor—for the maintenance and development of the proposed addition?
6. Will the library have permission to lend portions of the proposed collection to other libraries for exhibiting?

7. Is the new collection to be restricted in any manner concerning publication and use of photocopies or microfilm?
8. Does the donor require specific insurance coverage?
9. Will the owner transfer the copyright to the library, or if not who is to hold it?
10. Can the donor provide proof of legal ownership of the collection? (p. 120).

A carefully drafted deed agreement will take these items into consideration. If there are restrictions in the document transferring title, there should be time limits, after which the library is free to allow the public access to the materials. In the event that the deed does not refer to the matter of disposition, then legally, once the library has obtained title to the property, it is free to dispose of the materials as it sees fit.[8]

If the document granting title is a will, have *all* the heirs or owners of the materials agreed in writing to the transfer of ownership? *All* the owners must agree: more than one good collection has been lost at the last minute, after all negotiations had apparently been completed and the documents drawn up for signature, when one of the heirs to an estate refused to cooperate and release a collection.

The question of copyright also requires special attention.[9] Who holds the copyright to manuscript materials? Is the donor also *the creator* of the manuscripts? If not, then he or she can convey title to *the physical documents alone.* The donor cannot convey copyright ownership if he or she did not create the manuscripts without having obtained ownership from their author. Naturally, this issue can become complex should the question of publishing any part of those documents arise later. The ownership of the copyright should be stated in the deed of gift. Even if ownership of the copyright does not pass with the deed, the library can and should accept the physical ownership and hope that the party holding out may eventually change his or her mind. Barbara Kaiser has a different view and feels that "it is unrealistic to expect donors involved in creative careers to surrender their literary rights."[10]

## APPRAISAL OF GIFTS

The area of appraisals[11] is one in which most curators feel least confident, but it must be faced. And yet according to the Internal Revenue Service,

Appraisals are not always necessary. This is particularly true for minor items of property when you can easily determine the value of property by other means.[12]

In the vast majority of cases affecting special collections, however, appraising is pertinent. Appraisal value of gifts inevitably comes up when a donation is being made, and this value may be referred to in the donor's will. The general rule of special collections and libraries today is not to make an appraisal themselves and therefore not to commit themselves, orally or in writing. Most library associations have made explicit recommendations on this issue, including the "Statement on Appraisal of Gifts," issued by the Society of American Archivists in 1973:

> 1. The appraisal for tax purposes of a gift of manuscripts to a research institution, as well as the payment of related appraisal costs, is the responsibility of the donor, since it is the donor who receives the tax benefit.
> 2. As a matter of policy, a repository may: (a) inform its donors of provisions in the Internal Revenue Code pertaining to the appraisal of manuscript gifts; (b) provide, at the donor's request, auction records and dealers' catalogs available to the institution; (c) suggest appropriate professional appraisers; (d) provide administrative and processing services which will expedite the appraisal and assist the appraiser to make an accurate evaluation.
> 3. As a matter of policy, a repository should not: (a) alter its acceptance or archival processing standards because a prospective donor is interested in having his collection appraised; (b) agree, as the recipient institution, to appraise or estimate the market value of a manuscript collection or to endorse the monetary value assigned by a donor or professional appraiser either before or after the formal gift of the manuscripts to the institution; (c) discuss with prospective donors or publicize the appraisal value of individual manuscripts gifts which it has received; (d) permit the institution's name to be associated with appraisals made by its archival staff of materials donated to other repositories although the individual appraiser's credentials may reflect his institutional affiliation.[13]

On January 1, 1985, the Tax Reform Act of 1984 went into effect, introducing new changes. Among other things, appraisals for gifts valued over $5,000 (as opposed to the previous $200) are now mandatory. Libraries are required to provide a formal accounting to the IRS and to past donors about the disposition of gifts held less than two years. New penalties are levied against donors and appraisers for the *over-evaluation* of gifts. In addition, the IRS is cracking down on appraisers who have performed unsatisfactory work in the past, now preventing them from submitting subsequent appraisals for income tax purposes. Under the Tax Reform Act of 1984, a "qualified appraisal" must now include the following:

1. A description of the property appraised.
2. The fair market value of the property on the date of contribution and the specific basis for the valuation.
3. A statement that the appraisal was prepared for income tax purposes.
4. The signature and taxpayer identification number (TIN) of the appraiser.[14]

The new law also specifically states that *the appraiser cannot be the donee* or the taxpayer making the donation, nor can he or she be employed by or related to the donor.

The curator of special collections will also have to pay careful attention to a new provision of the 1984 Tax Reform Act pertaining to the disposition of donated property if it is sold, exchanged, or otherwise disposed of by your library within two years after its receipt. In such an event your institution must make a statement for the IRS and the original donor as well, giving the name, address, and TIN of the donor, a description of the property, the date of the contribution, the amount received on the disposition, and the date of such disposition. Institutions failing to comply with these provisions are now subject to annual penalties ranging from $50 to $50,000.

Another important change in the law states that appraisals will no longer be accepted if the fee is based on a percentage of the appraisal value of the property. A taxpayer who underpays taxes as a result of an inaccurate appraisal will have additional taxes to pay. And now a civil penalty of $1,000 can be imposed against an appraiser who aids and abets an understatement of tax liability by providing inaccurate appraisals. If the head of special collections does not remain alert when accepting a donation of books, the consequences may be rather unpleasant.

Although tax laws may change from year to year, the essence of the policies of libraries and related institutions does not. If the donor wants an appraisal, he or she has to obtain one, and though a value may have been given to a collection which the library has accepted, the acceptance of that collection does not constitute an endorsement of that value, and in fact the law now forbids any such endorsement.

Alfred Lane feels that if the material concerned is not worth appraising, a librarian may give an "estimate" or "approximate" value, with the understanding that the donor will be told that it is not an actual appraisal, and of course the entire transaction should be oral.[15] Columbia University's appraisal policy is a sound one:

> Donors are encouraged to consider having their gifts appraised for income or estate tax purposes. In general, the libraries follow the code on appraisals established by the American Booksellers Association. Because the Internal Revenue Service may consider a recipient library to be an interested party and disallow an evaluation made or paid for by the library, appraisal costs are normally borne by the donor. Upon request, the libraries will suggest appropriate persons or organizations to be consulted for professional appraisals. The acceptance of a gift which has been appraised by a disinterested party does not imply endorsement of the appraisal by the Libraries. When the value of the gift is nominal and does not warrant the cost of a professional appraisal, the Libraries may suggest guidelines or catalogs which the donor can use in determining his own evaluation.

Stanford University has established the following policy and procedures for the evaluation of all gifts to the library.

> Anyone connected with Stanford University is forbidden to appraise, for tax purposes, a gift to Stanford University. When an evaluation is required, the Gift & Exchange Division will initiate one of the following procedures:
> 1) The Gift & Exchange Division will set aside, for outside appraisal, significant gifts such as manuscripts, rare books, or large general collections;
> 2) The Gift & Exchange Division will inform donors of the publisher's list value or the subscription rate for small lots of current titles or periodicals. For out of print material you may use dust jacket prices, auction prices, or dealer catalogue prices. Sources must be cited and the donor must be told that this is *not* an appraisal for tax purposes.

Copies of all evaluations are then sent to the General Secretary's Office.

> Evaluations are made within the same tax year. The gift has to be physically at Stanford within the tax year claimed. Appraisals may be made the following year but the date of the gift must be stated.

Because of the high costs of insurance and appraisals, most valu-able rare books, manuscripts and archives in this country are neither appraised nor insured (when held in a library)—a disturbing fact. In-stead, librarians tend to feel that expense and effort should be made to provide for the safety and protection of their holdings against fire and theft—hence the introduction of sophisticated security systems in spe-cial collections and provision for a large fire-proof vault, as is done in the valuable Linnean Society's Library in London.[16]

Both the *Bookman's Price Index, A Guide to the Value of Rare and Other Out-of-Print Books,* published by the Gale Research Com-pany, and the older *American Book Prices Current,* published by Bancroft-Parkman, provide references for major book auctions in this country and Great Britian and should be a part of the curator's reference section.

## Gift Donation and Acceptance Forms

Every library has its own form of agreement for accepting the donation of books and mancuscripts. The following is used by Stanford:

The Board of Trustees of The Leland Stanford, Jr. University acknowledges that it has accepted from


a gift to the Stanford University Libraries of


Books and other materials for the University Libraries may, in the discretion of the Director of University Libraries, be incorporated into the Collections, exchanged for other materials, or sold, the proceeds being used for the benefit of the University Libraries.

This gift is absolute and irrevocable.

In witness whereof the donor has subscribed his name hereto and the Board of Trustees has caused its name to be subscribed this _____ day of _____, 19

_____
DONOR

---

DONOR'S ADDRESS

The Board of Trustees of The Leland Stanford Junior
University.

BY _____


The essential words in the form are, of course, "absolute and irrevocable."

Stanford also covers the option of having a book or manuscript
collection on loan during a donor's lifetime, and then having it become
Stanford property upon the death of the donor. The following "deposit" form is used for this purpose:


DEPOSIT-GIFT AGREEMENT


    It is agreed on this _____ day of _____,
19___ , between _____ and the BOARD OF
TRUSTEES OF THE LELAND STANFORD JUNIOR UNIVERSITY
that the Manuscripts Division of the Department of
Special Collections, Stanford University Libraries,
on behalf of the BOARD OF TRUSTEES OF THE LELAND
STANFORD JUNIOR UNIVERSITY, will accept the following
described papers and materials, heretofore and now
the property of _____,
on (temporary/permanent) loan, and with the understanding
that the title of all of said papers and materials will
become the property of the BOARD OF TRUSTEES OF THE
LELAND STANFORD JUNIOR UNIVERSITY pursuant to the
provisions of the Will of _____,
or in the option of _____,
by prior intervivos gifts of all or any part or
portion of said described papers and materials at
such time or times during his/her lifetimes as
_____ may elect:

(DESCRIPTION OF THE PAPERS AND MATERIALS IS INCLUDED HERE)


    It is further agreed that the said described papers
and materials shall be arranged and catalogued and a guide
or register to the said papers and materials will be

prepared and the collection reported to the National
Union Catalog of Manuscript Collections.

It is further agreed that the said described papers
and materials shall be placed in protective containers
and shelved in locked stack areas within the said
Department of Special Collections and made available to
researchers on request in a supervised reading room.

In the discretion of Stanford University Libraries
such parts or portions of said described papers and
materials from time to time may be loaned for exhibition
purposes to responsible, reputable and reliable institutions and agencies, provided, however, that proper
protective facilities are available and employed and
that the said papers and materials so loaned are fully
insured against loss or damage from whatever cause
arising during the time said papers and materials are
not in the custody of the Stanford University Libraries.

_____
Signature (Name)

THE BOARD OF TRUSTEES OF THE
LELAND STANFORD JUNIOR UNIVERSITY

By_____

Its_____

Various universities suggest specific forms for the transfer of testa-
mentary gifts and donations and the three following bequest forms
currently used by Yale are as succinct as any I have come across:[17]

FORM FOR GIFT TO THE UNIVERSITY FOR ITS GENERAL PURPOSES

I bequeath to _____ University, ___(City)___, ___(State)___,
$. . . . . . to be used (or, the net income, including
so much of the appreciation in value as the Corporation
of the University may appropriate from the amount determined by it to exist, to be used) at the discretion of
the Corporation of the University.

FORM FOR GIFT TO THE UNIVERSITY FOR A SPECIFIC PURPOSE

I bequeath to _____ University, ___(City)___, ___(State)___,
$. . . . . . to be used (or, the net income, including
so much of the appreciation in value as the Corporation
of the University may appropriate from the amount deter-

mined by it to exist, to be used) for the following
(Here specify the purpose, such as the university
libraries or a special collection).  If at any time in
the judgment of the Corporation of the University it
is impossible or impracticable to carry out exactly
the above purpose in the above manner, a purpose and
manner as near as is practicable to the above purpose
and manner shall be determined by the Corporation of
the University.

FORM FOR GIFT TO THE UNIVERSITY OF TANGIBLE PROPERTY
FOR THE LIBRARY

I bequeath to _____ University, ___(City__, ___(State)__,
the following described property, said property or the
proceeds of the disposition thereof, if any, to be used
for the benefit of the _____ University Library: (Here
describe the property).

Following is the "Universal Gift Form" agreement drawn up by the
Committee on Manuscripts Collections of the Rare Books and Manuscripts Section of the Association of College and Research Libraries:[18]

UNIVERSAL GIFT FORM

(Board of Trustees of
the
Anonymous Athenaeum)

I/We hereby give, transfer, and deliver all of my/our
right, title and interest in and to the property described
below to the (Board of Trustees of the Anonymous Athenaeum)
as an unrestricted gift and dedicate to the public without
restriction and thereby place in the public domain whatever
literary rights I/we may possess to this property.

Dated this _____ day of _____, 19____:

1. _____
   Signature

   _____
   Address

2. _____
   Signature

      Address
_____

3.  _____
      Signature

      _____
      Address

The (Board of Trustees of the Anonymous Athenaeum) hereby accepts and acknowledges as an unrestricted gift to the (Library of the Anonymous Athenaeum) the collection described below and agrees to administer it in accordance with its established policies.

Dated this _____ day of _____, 19____ :

Accepted by: _____
                    Signature

                _____
                    Title

Description of the collection: _____

_____

_____

## Exchanges and Cooperation

Exchanges may be carried out through agreements with individual libraries, or through the Duplicate Exchange Union, or with foreign libraries through the U.S. Book Exchange. Some libraries, for instance, may have hundreds of exchange agreements across the country, although as a rule exchanges play only a minor role, compared, say, to gifts, in the case of special collections. When such exchanges do take place, one must consider whether it might be cheaper for the library to purchase the books than to spend time, and money on the transactions. Exchanges require establishing the current value of the books in question, a value which the exchanging library must match. (In the past this was done on a title-by-title basis.)[19] It is Alfred Lane's opinion that "the most efficient and effective exchange program" is one made between individual institutions.[20]

Another, looser, form of exchange is a cooperative agreement with other libraries to facilitate their passing on to you anything that might meet your needs but does not apply to their subject areas. Your library, by the same token, will pass items on to them. This rarely amounts to an even exchange of materials, and there is no attempt to establish reciprocal values. Indeed, a reciprocal exchange may not occur for years. This loose sort of cooperation has been put into effect throughout the country, generally among archives as opposed to rare books.

## Endowments

Some special collections departmetns in libraries have no budget of their own, and those that do often receive less—significantly less— than twenty thousand dollars a year for acquisitions, preservation, and supplies. The largest special collections departments in the United States, with six- or seven-digit budgets, are inevitably the best endowed ones, such as the Beinecke at Yale, the Widener at Harvard, and the Newberry.

Endowments are generally made by individuals on their own behalf, or as a memorial in someone's honor, although foundations and corporations are also sources. Endowments are usually encouraged initially by an influential library or university administrator in the course of social events, or perhaps directly by the Gifts and Exchange Office. Prominent alumni are a normal source of such endowments. Universities generally ask for the widest possible latitude in the use of such funds, as exemplified in the following addition by Yale Unviersity to its general purpose gift form:[21]

### FORM CONCERNING INVESTMENTS

The University is authorized in its discretion to mingle the property at any time constituting the investments of the fund with investments representing other Endowment Funds of the University, and in case of such mingling to allocate income to the Fund at the rate at which income is allocated from time to time by the University to such other mingled Endowment Funds.

Endowments are naturally sought by special collections because they provide a separate, guaranteed annual revenue which makes the curator independent of regular library budgetary control and restrictions.[22] For example, if the usual budget for a special collection is $15,000, but an emergency occurs and the comptroller or library director is forced to reduce the allocated funds by, say, $5,000, the curator's entire program for that year may be in jeopardy. This can never happen with endowed revenues. Nevertheless, if the fund is invested in the stock market, the annual endowment revenue will be subject to fluctuations. Indeed, some libraries have had to retrench during the recent recession as a result of such fluctuations, though the funds generally rebound. A prestigious collection easily attracts more funds, but for the medium-sized or smaller university libraries which have no famous collection, it is obviously more difficult. In such cases, the curator must take other routes—through local bibliophiles, for example. If a Rockefeller or Carnegie cannot be found locally, perhaps the curator can find a dozen individuals who are willing to contribute smaller amounts to form a single endowment. In the final analysis, however, the separate endowment fund is the curator's best bet.

## References

1. Even when the document concerned transfers full ownership of a collection, some state university libraries are enjoined from selling any materials in their library, regardless of provenance. (One cannot sell "state" property in such cases.)
2. On the subject of gifts and bequests, see: American Library Association, "Statement of Policy Regarding Gifts and Bequests to Libraries, Adopted in 1939," *American Libraries,* 2 (July 1971), 721-22; Alfred H. Lane, *Gifts and Exchange Manual* (Westport, Conn: Greenwood Press, 1980), and also his article, "Gifts and Exchanges: Practicalities and Problems," *Library Resources and Technical Services,* 14 (Winter 1970), 92-97; L.N. Gerhardt, "On Gifts," *School Library Journal,* 29 (Oct. 1982), 65; and Anne E. Prentice et al., "Gifts, Grants and Bequests," in *Library Trustee* (New York, 1972), 66-71. See also W. V. Dole's "Gifts and Block Purchases: Are They Profitable?" *Library Acquisitions: Practice and Theory,* 7, No. 3 (1983), 247-54.
3. Trudy H. Peterson, "Gift and the Deed," *American Archivist,* 42, No. 1 (Jan. 1979), 61-66.
4. Alfred Lane of Columbia University points out a pitfall to be avoided at all costs when the will is being prepared: the use of the term "books." E.g., the will states the heir is to have a choice of "500 books" from the collection

before turning it over to the library in question. Oddly enough there is no clear definition of this term. Is a book a single volume or a title? If it is a title (which encompasses several volumes), are all the volumes counted separately, or as "one book"? For example, would the 46-volume work of A. E. Montémont, *Histoire Universelle des Voyages Effectués par Mer et par Terre dans les Cinq Parties du Monde,* be considered "one book" or "46 books"?

5. Barbara J. Kaiser, "Problems with Donors of Contemporary Collections," *The American Archivist,* 32, No. 2 (April 1969), 105.

6. Alfred Lane, "Gifts and Exchanges: Practicalities and Problems," p. 94.

7. *Ibid.*

8. Trudy Peterson, p. 65.

9. K. Winn, "Common Law, Copyright and the Archivist," *The American Archivist,* 37 (July 1974), 375-86.

10. Barbara J. Kaiser, p. 105.

11. See: D. R. Briggs, "Gift Appraisal Policy in Large Research Libraries," *College and Research Libraries,* 9 (Nov. 1958), 505-07; H. Finch, "Gifts, Appraisals and Taxes," *Cornell University Library Bulletin,* 189 (May 1974), 7-10; D. Lamer and G. Anderson, "Gift Books and Appraisals," *College and Research Libraries,* 40 (Sept. 1979), 440-43; Thomas W. Leonhardt, "Gift Appraisals: A Practical Approach," *Library Acquisitions: Practice and Theory,* 3, No. 2 (1979), 77-79; D. V. Osier, "Appraising Library Material Donations: An Explanation of the Appraisal Process for Libraries," *Minnesota Libraries,* 26 (Autumn 1979), 477-83; W. Z. Schenck, "Evaluation and Valuing Gift Materials," *Library Acquisitions,* 6, No. 1 (1982), 33-40.

12. Quoted from the IRS's *Valuation of Donated Property,* 1978 Edition, IRS Publication 561.

13. "Standards on Appraisal of Gifts," *The American Archivist,* 37, No. 1 (Jan. 1974), 154-55. Compare this with the "Statement on Appraisal of Gifts" adopted by the Association of College and Research Libraries, published in *Guidelines on Manuscripts And Archives* (Chicago: Association of College and Research Libraries, 1977), p. 3 and also in the *College and Research Libraries News,* 34, No. 3 (March 1979), 49, which are similar.

14. See John R. Payne, "A Closer Eye On Appraisals," *College & Research Libraries News* (Feb. 1985), 52-56. Reprinted by permission of the American Library Association. See also K.W. Rendell, "New Appraisal Rules; Congress May Restore Tax Benefits," *AB Bookman's Weekly,* 74 (Nov. 19, 1984), 3611 *et seq.*

15. Alfred Lane, "Gifts and Exchanges: Practicalities and Problems," 92-96.

16. Interview with Gavin Bridson, Bibliographer of the Linnean Society's Library in London (April 1983).

17. Rutherford D. Rogers, "Report of the University Librarian, July 1980-June 1981, *Bulletin of Yale University,* 78, No. 1 (Jan. 1982), inside back cover. "These forms should not be construed as the last statement on the matter."—per John A. Wilkinson, Office of the Secretary, Yale University, in letter to the author, Nov. 9, 1983.

18. Published in the ACRL's *Guidelines on Manuscripts and Archives* (Chicago: Association of College and Research Libraries, 1977), p. 10. ACRL's "Statement on Legal Title" is a contract transferring property and rights from one party to another, published on p. 4 of *Guidelines on Manuscripts and Archives:*

### STATEMENT ON LEGAL TITLE

1. Every library should acquire proper and legal title to all gifts of books, manuscripts, and other materials, which have significant monetary value. It is recognized, however, (a) that it is often impossible to acquire title to collections many years after they have been received by the library; (b) that frequently, where small collections of materials are involved, the donor may not be certain exactly where title rests; and (c) that when single items or very small collections are involved, donors often do not wish to become involved in library gift procedures.

2. Many libraries still accept temporary deposits. As a general principle, such gifts ordinarily should not be accepted unless (a) the library has reason to believe that a temprorary deposit is the only way in which the material is likely to be preserved; or (b) the library has reason to believe that a temporary deposit will in time be changed to a permanent gift; or (c) except where ownership of corporate records is governed by state and/or federal regulations.

3. Ordinarily transfer of legal title by gift is accomplished by a properly executed form, variously described as "Instrument of Gift" or "Certificate of Gift." This form should include the following: (a) name and address of the donor; (b) description of the gift; (c) statement of transfer of legal title, and where possible and applicable, copyrights and literary  rights; (d) any restrictions; (e) directions concerning disposal of unwanted items.

The form must be (1) signed and dated by the donor and (2) witnessed and dated by another party who is neither related to the donor nor employed by the institution receiving the gift.

An additional evidence of proof would be the notarization of the donor's and witnesses' signatures.

19. Lane, "Gifts and Exchanges: Practicalities and Problems," 92-96.

20. *Ibid.,* p. 96.

21. *Bulletin of Yale University,* 78, No. 1 (Jan. 1982), inside back cover.

22. See also the discussion on possible integration of manuscripts, archives, and rare books in four articles in the November 1984 issue of *College & Research Libraries,* 45, No. 6: Donald Farren, "Integration or Separation: A Preface," pp. 435-36; Clifton H. Jones, "Remarks on the Integration of Special Collections," pp. 437-41; William L. Joyce, "Rare Books, Manuscripts, and Other Special Collections Materials: Integration or Separation?" pp. 442-45; and Richard C. Berner, "Manuscript Collections, Archives, and Special Collections: Their Relationships," pp. 446-49. Some of the ramifications of the integration of special collections within the mainstream of library holdings are rather disturbing.

# 8

# The Annual Report

The annual report is the summation of the activities of the special collections department and should reflect them in considerable detail. Many curators dread preparing it and postpone this task as long as possible, but if a special current annual report file is maintained on a regular basis, the essential data will have accumulated painlessly throughout the year, and the curator needs only to digest, analyze, and collate the materials. The importance of the annual report should not be underestimated. When the annual budget is considered and weighed, the departmental annual report will be consulted. When the curator calls for an increase of staff, it is this report that will be studied.

The variety of annual reports issued by libraries and special collections departments, in content, format, and physical appearance, is astonishing. A library's general annual report is usually a surprisingly brief document, frequently ranging from twenty to sixty pages, and is as a whole much more general in focus than the annual report of any one library department, as for instance in the case of most special collections' annual reports which are naturally longer and more detailed and statistical. The reports of some private libaries are produced in a large format ($8\frac{1}{2} \times 11$) as in the case of the Newberry, on expensive paper, with numerous photographs of staff, facilities, and sample acquisitions. Others are in a much smaller format such as that of the Henry E. Huntington Library and Art Gallery of San Marino, Calif., which is almost half the size of the former. University library reports are equally varied. The University of Minnesota Libraries come out with about a twenty-page report of inexpensive photocopy held together by a single staple, whereas the University Libraries of the University of South Carolina publishes a fifty-page report bound with a sturdy, printed red cover ($8 \times 10$). Yale produces one of the finest reports published anywhere, within the printed blue covers of the *Bulletin of Yale University* (measuring only 5 × 8) with over sixty closely printed pages and no photographs or illustrations. Princeton University Library in the mid-1970s came out with perhaps the shortest and one of the least informative annual reports, covering less than a dozen pages, stapled together, although Stanford's 1980-1981 report was not much more informative. Regardless of the form, it is the total number of the library's departments' annual reports which provides the library director with the information for the general library annual report.

If the physical formats vary considerably, the contents of the annual reports do even more. Although the Henry E. Huntington Library of San Marino comprises in addition an art gallery and botanical garden, it is essentially a research library as its Annual Report's table of contents reflects:[1]

PEOPLE AND PROGRESS.
(Indicates number of scholars, their work, and photos of staff.)
THE ART GALLERY
THE BOTANICAL GARDEN
THE LIBRARY
1. *New Acquisitions:*
   a. Americana
   b. English Manuscripts and Books
   c. Continental Books
   d. Print Collection
   e. Special Gifts
   f. Reference Books
2. *Departments of the Library:*
   a. Department of Manuscripts
   b. Department of Rare Books
   c. Department of Prints
   d. Department of Readers Services
   e. Department of Photographic Reproductions
   f. The Bindery (bound and repaired)
APPENDIXES
   1. The Staff
   2. Special Exhibitions
   3. Research Seminars (dates, subjects, etc.)
   4. Visiting Research Scholars Who Hold Grants
   5. Publications by Members of the Staff
   6. Professional Activities of Members of the Staff

7. Publications of the Huntington Library
8. Special Events (e.g., previews of exhibitions)
9. Donors to the Library and Art Gallery
10. Donors to the Botanical Garden

The report concludes with the financial situation—the balance sheet of assets and liabilities, and the statement of operating fund income and expenditure.

*The University of Minnesota's University Libraries Annual Report for 1979/80* includes:

GENERAL INTRODUCTION: Five-Year Review
  I. COLLECTIONS (Numerical increase in acquisitions, with no mention of special collections, nor of any titles of works acquired, or their significance.)
 II. SERVICES (The increase in hours of service of all the libraries and includes "Special collections exhibits, programs, and catalogs were a major continuing activity in the Wilson Library. There "were exhibits and programs on the history of U.S. maps, the Hench Collection, private Minnesota presses, Evangelos P. Papanoutsos, the the English Ballad, and Defoe."
III. OPERATIONS
 IV. PERSONNEL
  V. FACILITIES
 VI. ORGANIZING AND PLANNING
VII. STATE, REGIONAL, AND NATIONAL RELATIONS
VIII. A BRIEF LOOK AHEAD
     TABLES:
     1. Five-Year Comparison—Basic Data
     2. Budgets (S & W, SE & E, Acquisitions, Binding)
     3. Collection Size (Catalogued vols., Government Publications, manuscripts, maps, etc.)
     4. Public Service:
        a. Service Hours
        b. Circulation
        c. Photocopies
        d. Interlibrary loans
     5. Processing (Titles catalogued, original/copy, acquisitions, serials, volumes bound, gifts, archives)
     6. Personnel

In the mid-1970's, the University of California at Berkeley produced a five-year *Annual Report for the General Library* and covered:

PREFACE
THE COLLECTIONS (statistical analysis and effect of inflation)
LIST OF SIGNIFICANT ACQUISITIONS (chiefly rare books)
PHYSICAL FACILITIES
INTERNAL ORGANIZATIONAL DEVELOPMENTS
PERSONNEL CONCERNS
LIBRARY SERVICES
THE FUTURE
CONCLUDING OBSERVATIONS
ADMINISTRATIVE STAFF
LIST OF SIGNIFICANT EXHIBITIONS
STATISTICAL TABLES
(Contains the University Library Collection, breakdown by each individual library—Main Library, Bancroft, Moffitt, etc.—Data on Other Collections—manuscripts, maps, microforms, etc.—a breakdown of branch or departmental library collections, e.g. Biology, East Asiatic, music, physical sciences, etc., and finally, circulation data "Document Delivery Systems."

Perhaps the biggest surprise of all was to be found in *Stanford's University Libraries Annual Report 1980–1981.* This begins with a summation of the year by the director, reflecting trends, changes, the successful fund-raising campaign, and then listing some of the year's donors. The next eighteen pages list "Selected Gifts to the Collections," consisting chiefly of rare books, manuscripts, and signed first editions of works. The final two pages of this thirty-four-page report list further selected donors of library materials, the Executive Committee of the Associates of the Stanford University Libraries, Members of the Academic Council Committee on Libraries, the Visiting Committee to the Stanford University Libraries, and finally gives the names of the five highest officers of the Stanford University Libraries. It is nothing short of staggering to think that such an excellent system of libraries could come out with an annual report which failed to discuss budgetary details, the breakdown of collection holdings and acquisitions, cataloging, conservation and preservation, a list of library publications, staff and staff activities, or exhibitions.

Stanford's *Annual Report* contrasts with *The Report of the University Librarian, July 1980–1981,* which appeared in the January issue of the *Bulletin of Yale University,* and which is probably the finest of its kind. This sixty two-page *Annual Report* by Rutherford Rogers includes the following categories:

Introduction
Inflation
Acquisitions
Other gifts
Use of the Collections
Organization of the Collections
Projects
Preservation
Space
Special Developments and Activities
Exhibits
Publications
People
Comparative Financial Data
Additions to the Library's Endowment and Expendable Funds
Additions to Principal of Established Funds
Advisers to the Library
Statistics:
   Accessions
   Accessions of Microforms
   Serial Titles Received
   Cataloguing
   Circulation
   Conservation
   Preparation
   Preservation
   Interlibrary Lending and Borrowing
   Manuscripts (received, accessioned, catalogued, etc.)
   Volumes in School & Department Libraries

This report is worth examining closely. For example, of the sixty-two pages, nineteen are concerned in detail with outstanding acquisitions, while another dozen pages cover statistics, some of which are concerned also with conservation and preservation.

    Under the subject of acquisitions, Rogers goes into considerable detail about donated manuscripts, papers, personal writings, and books, including libraries purchased. While most acquisitions tend to fall in the category of special collections, other areas include art and architecture, microfiliming projects, music, geology, etc. Despite this

Stacks of the Beinecke Rare Book and Manuscript Library, Yale University. Courtesy of Yale University Office of Public Information

outstanding section, this still does not relate the emphasis which Yale places, and the pride it takes, in *quality acquisitions*. Many paragraphs of this third of the *Annual Report* include those rare books and manuscripts going directly to the Beinecke. In addition to thousands of valuable letters, Rogers mentions the following Beinecke acquisition, and it should be kept in mind that this is not the annual report for the Beinecke, but simply the emphasis placed on rare books in the general library report.

> In December, at Sotheby's, the Beinecke Library successfully bid on the galley proofs of Walter de la Mare's *Desert Islands and Robinson Crusoe,* with copious autograph revisions by the author. The Library bought eleven letters from Norman Douglas to the Terence Holliday, full of interesting details about the publication and distribution of two of his books (*experiments* and *Birds and Beasts of the Greek Anthology*), as well as 200 letters from Douglas to David Jeffreys whose collection of Douglas's books and manuscripts was acquired several years ago.

The Beinecke Library also bought twenty titles by Defoe, Fielding, James Hurdis, John Holwell, Elizabeth Rowe, and others, printed in Great Britain during the eighteenth century, five German almanacs, Andreas Rüdiger's *Philosophia pragmatica* (Leipzig, 1723), and Jacopo Morelli's *Monumenti veneziani di varia letteratura* (Venice, 1796), a handsomely printed literary collection containing four letters by Memo and a letter from Galileo to the Doge of Venice proposing military uses for his telescope.

The Beinecke Library was able to add three new letters to the Boswell collection. One is to Boswell from his tenant Andrew Dalrymple, who had been imprisoned for his failure to pay his rent and who in this letter pleads for a bond, with two named securities, to enable him to obtain his freedom and earn the money to repay his debt. Below Dalrymple's signature Boswell wrote a note agreeing to the terms (but not requiring a bond) and added: 'He is the first of my tenants I ever imprisoned and I hope he will behave better in time to come.'

The other two letters are from Boswell's brother Thomas David to their brother John, telling him of the death of their mother (January 11, 1766) and from Boswell's son Alexander (Sandy) at Eton, to the estate agent Andrew Gibb (November 15, 1791), enquiring about affairs at Auchinleck and asking to have his gun sent to him.

The Beinecke Library bought 4 *Short-title Catalogue* items, including a fine copy of *The Countess of Pembroke's Arcadia* (London, 1613) to replace a very imperfect one; and 8 Wing-period titles. Also purchased was a splendid copy of the most attractive of Spanish writing books, prepared by Jose de Casanova, a teacher of calligraphy; this was printed in Madrid in 1650. Casanova's presentation of the usual historical and technical information is accompanied by plates showing alphabets in Gothic and Italian scripts, Spanish Ronde, and the Lettera Bastarda which he was influential in introducing into Spain.

The 22 sixteenth-century books that the Beinecke Library bought were printed in Europe on a variety of subjects from Claude Guichard's book on burial custons (Lyon, 1581) to Ugolini Verino's account of Renaissance Florence (Paris, 1583) and to Johann Boemus's first systematic comparative study of cultures (Augsburg, 1520).

Perhaps the rarest of the sixteenth-century purchases was Geiler von Kaiserberg's *Das irrig Schaf* (Strassbourg, ca. 1510), a very fine copy of his allegorical sermons which includes the earliest illustrated version of the Cinderella story.

Four incunabula were bought: 2 Savonarolas at the Sexton sale, a very scarce edition of Marcus Manilius's *Astronomicon* (Rome, 1484) and, with Library Associates funds, a copy of the *Legenda aurea* of Jacobus de Voragine (Augsburg, Gunther Zainer, ca. 1474). This gathering of the lives of the saints was so popular that almost 60 editions were published between

1471 and 1499; of these Yale has eleven, beginning with 1476. The special feature of the 1474 Zainer edition is the series of 163 vivid woodcuts depicting the saints. Zainer had used these woodcuts in his first edition of the *Legenda aurea* published in German in 1471 (only one complete copy in America) and then used them again in this Latin edition. As one of the earliest attempts to illustrate an entire book, this edition is of considerable interest to the historians of printing and of woodcut illustration. There is no recorded copy in the British Library or in the libraries of Belgium, France, or Italy.

Beinecke Library purchases also included two pre 1600 manuscripts. The first is by a little-known Flemish writer, Wouter of Verviers, and is an explication of the text of Porphyry. It was written in the late fifteenth century and is bound with a copy of the third edition of Walter Burley's *Exposition in artem veterem Porphyrii et Aristotelis* (Venice, 1481), a commentary on older texts which may have set the pattern for a medieval method of scientific investigation.

The second is a collection of accounts of early travels of English merchant adventurers in Russia and the Middle East; the most important of these accounts is by Anthony Keninson who, during his stay in Russia from 1557 to 1561, was closely associated with Czar Ivan IV.[2]

But the general report of the library does not end with those nineteen pages of acquisitions, for under "Other Gifts" lists are made of various gifts presented to the library, and it provides a good example of a special bequest made to Yale years earlier, but which had just come to it now.

While the Kenneth Scott Latourette bequest was made in 1965, it is appropriate to report that the estate came to the library during this year. Valued in excess of $500,000, this estate has now established a restricted book fund for the acquisition of mission and other historical materials from third world countries. The continued prominence of the Day Missions Library is thus assured by this substantial gift.[3]

Under the category Use of the Collections, two items affect special collections. "The number of visits to the Manuscripts and Archives Collection rose almost 40 percent, from 3,514, to 4,919. . . . "[4] And then referring to the rare books collection:

The number of visitors to the Beinecke Library rose substantially from the previous year, up from 84,239 to 90,781. The number of books used in the reading room rose from 14,107 in 1979-1980 to 16,050 in 1980-1981, and the number of researchers increased from 7,698 to 8,872.[5]

Under the heading Projects, two of interest were mentioned: 1. The Preservation and Subject Guide Project, and 2. Automated Cataloguing of Manuscripts and Realted Projects.[6]

Once again, now under the heading Preservation, Rogers strikes out to bolster this necessary adjunct to the library:

> The number of volumes sent to the Preservation Division was up this year by 41 percent (6,249 this year and 4,439 last) while the number of volumes processed rose by 43 percent (4,542 this year and 3,186 last) which is still 27 percent fewer volumes processed than in 1978-1979. The number of volumes withdrawn without replacement rose by 35 percent (603 this year and 448 last); the number replaced by all means increased by 14 percent (from 1,423 to 1,620); and Conservation staff repaired and rebound 54 percent more volumes (686 this year and 446 last).[7]

Under Publications, Yale again highlights the Library's special holdings:

> Several important and long-awaited publications appeared during the year. In 1938 Thomas Mann gave, through Joseph W. Angell, eighty-four leaves of rejected and revised pages from his most famous novel, *Der Zauberberg,* and from then until now Mann scholars have awaited the transcription by the late James F. White that was finally published in *Thomas-Mann-Studien,* volume IV, 1980.
>
> The year also saw the publication of the two major works, *Dickens and Dickensiana, a catalogue of the Richard Gimbel Collection in the Yale University Library,* by John B. Podeschi, and *A Catalogue of the Cary Collection of Playing Cards,* four volumes, prepared by William B. Keller.
>
> *The Yale Edition of Horace Walpole's Correspondence,* 40, 41, and 42 were published in December, 1980, containing the remainder of the known letters from and to Horace Walpole. It is anticipated that "Additions and Corrections" and approximately five volumes of Index will be published by early 1983, bringing to completion the vast enterprise begun by Wilmarth S. Lewis in 1937.[8]

These works were published by the Library and are not to be confused with the regular publications of Yale University Press. And it is interesting to note that this entire section and the others cited could also have been included in the annual report of the curator of special collections, underlining Yale's dedication to special collections.

Under Comparative Financial Data, the Library has singled out such items as preservation, endowment funds, rare books and manuscripts (see Figure 1). Under Additions to the Library's Endowment and Expendable Funds are listed newly acquired funds during that year, usually of a restrictive nature, for example the Latourette mentioned earlier, which are to be used exclusively for the purchase of printed and manuscript sources on Protestant, Roman Catholic, and Eastern Orthodox foreign missions.

These examples are from Additions to Principal of Established Funds:[9]

> BEINECKE RARE BOOK FUND
> Edwin J. Beinecke Trust, $250,000
> Royalties $262.50
>
> BEINECKE RARE BOOK AND MANUSCRIPT LIBRARY
> MAINTENANCE FUND
> Beinecke Foundation, $174,150.
>
> CARRIE S. BEINECKE FUND, NO. 1
> Carrie S. Beinecke Twenty-Year Trust,
> $119,313.10.
>
> BOSWELL PAPER EDITING FUND
> Professor Chester Chapin, $500; W. Curtis Carrol Davis, $1,000; Charles Beecher Hogan (B.A., 1928, M.A., 1933), $1,000; Mr. and Mrs. Maurice Jacobs, $100; Mrs. William Peyton May, $500; Andrew W. Mellon Foundation, $65,000; Arthur G. Rippey, $250; Warren H. Smith, $250; Dr. Josephine Wiseman, $100.
>    Royalties, $456.53.

The Boswell Papers Fund is a fine example of how donations can vary in size; in this case, from as little as $100 to $65,000. No donor is too unimportant for Yale, and the Library well realizes how quickly they all add up. They are named not only in the annual report of the curator for special collections, but in the library's general report as well, and Yale's annual report lists seven pages of such donations.

FIGURE I   Financial Data, 1980–81

| *Summary of Expenses* | |
|---|---:|
| Salaries | $ 6,452,211 |
| Wages | 551,730 |
| Employee Benefits | 1,082,397 |
| Acquisitions | 3,026882 |
| Binding and Preservation Supplies | 279,521 |
| Equipment | 189,108 |
| Operating Costs | 1,916,237 |
| Total | $13,498,086 |

| *Sources of Funds* | |
|---|---:|
| General Appropriation | $ 9,094,001 |
| Endowment Funds | 2,297,981 |
| Gifts, Grants, and Other | 2,106,104 |
| | $13,498,086 |

| *Types of Acquisitions* | |
|---|---:|
| *Monographs* | *$ 1,060,207* |
| *Rare Books* | *373,896* |
| *Manuscripts* | *137,927* |
| *Maps* | *2,896* |
| *Serials* | *1,334,780* |
| *Microtext* | *86,269* |
| *Other Acquisitions (photographs, musical scores, coins, etc.)* | *30,907* |
| | *$ 3,026,882* |

Accessions to the library are listed under the following categories: purchase, gift, exchange PL 480, by transfers from other libraries, each category broken down in turn as in the following case for:

*Added by purchase*

| | |
|---|---|
| Books and pamphlets | 13,603 |
| Serials | 18,542 |
| Records | 1,156 |
| Tapes | —— |
| Maps | 133 |

The Accessions of Microforms is given a separate page of its own and uses the following categories, e.g., for the Main Library:

| | |
|---|---|
| Microfilms (reels) | 3,494 |
| Microprints (sheets) | 34,852 |
| Microfiches (sheets) | 30,775 |
| Machine-readable data files | —— |

Once again Cataloguing has several pages, broken down into two general categories, Main Library, and then School and Department Libraries. The following example is for the main Library, 1980-81:

Main Library
  Titles catalogued

| | |
|---|---|
| Books and pamphlets | 64,861 |
| Serials | 6,671 |
| Microtexts | 1,359 |
| Records | —— |

Then using the same four sub-categories, Titles Catalogued is followed by:

Titles recataloged
Titles reclassed
Volumes cataloged
Volumes recataloged
Volumes reclassed

Under Circulation, the following general categories are considered: Sterling Memorial Library, Cross Campus Library, Beinecke Rare Book and Manuscript Library, School and Department Libraries, and Circulation Totals. Under the Beinecke we thus have:

Beinecke Rare Books and Manuscript Library:
  Volumes used in the building 17,858

The Yale Libraries are one of the very few in the United States to issue a separate page on the status of Conservation, and though they cover three sets of years, I quote only from 1980-81:[10]

*Conservation*

| | |
|---|---:|
| Books | 1,369 |
| Protective Cases | 369 |
| Paper | 1,135 |

*Binding*

| | |
|---|---:|
| Pamphlets: | |
| Gaylord binding | Discontinued |
| Staples | 2,760 |
| Hollinger | 12,241 |
| Paper covered | 320 |
| Hollinger-Hinge | 62 |
| Volumes Rebound | 55 |
| Temporary bindings | —— |
| Portfolio/Boxes | —— |

*Repairs*

| | |
|---|---:|
| Volumes | —— |
| Inserts | 121 |
| Pockets | 210 |
| Pages mended | 136 |

This is followed by two related fields, Preparation and Preservation:[11]

*Main Library*

| | |
|---|---:|
| Volumes labeled | 115,272 |
| Loose plates hand-marked | 5,180 |
| Volumes plated | 66,359 |
| Volumes plate-stamped | 18,827 |
| Issue slips applied | 80,446 |
| Identification stamps | 164,266 |
| Volumes revised | 90,341 |
| Labels removed | 5,177 |
| Bookplates removed | 70 |
| Boxes replaced | 21 |
| Plates and titles typed | 1,157 |
| CCL book pockets applied | 8,872 |
| Serials bound commercially | 8,091 |
| Monographs bound commercially | 16,408 |

We then come to Library's Preservation statistics:[12]

| | |
|---|---:|
| Volumes in poor condition received | 6,374 |
| Volumes sent directly to Preparations | 125 |
| Volumes sent to Preservation | 6,249 |
| Volumes processed by Preservation | 4,542 |
| Volumes in process | 1,795 |
| Volumes awaiting processing | 6,014 |

And the following form for presenting statistics on Manuscripts:[13]

*Main Library*
Linear feet (items, pages, etc.):

| | |
|---|---:|
| Received | 8,011 |
| Accessioned | 10 |
| Cataloged | 2,143 |
| Labeled | —— |
| Items to readers | 159,470 |
| Copies made | 204,209 |
| Copies of MSS elsewhere | 1,014 |

*School and Department Libraries*
Linear feet (items, pages, etc.):

| | |
|---|---:|
| Received | 20,757 |
| Accessioned | 87 |
| Cataloged | 35 |
| Labeled | 357 |
| Items to readers | 664 |
| Copies made | 14,000 |
| Copies of MSS elsewhere | 9,653 |

If Yale's General Annual Report seems almost as detailed on special collections as the Departmental Report on that subject, other libraries follow different formats. The Houghton Library of Harvard issues a long annual report (usually around eighty pages) entitled *The Houghton Library Report of Accessions for the Year.* Though the one I am discussing dates from the mid-1960's, its format is still valid. The Houghton lists, in fourteen separate categories, a report on every title acquired that year, and these are broken down as follows:[14]

European Books and Manuscripts of the Sixteenth Century and Earlier.
  This includes the name of the donor or seller, what is acquired and its
  significance
English Books to 1640
European Books and Manuscripts of the Seventeenth Century
Seventeenth Century Science
English Books and Manuscripts, 1641-1700
European Books and Manuscripts of the Eighteenth Century
Eighteenth Century English Books and Manuscripts
Americana to 1800
Nineteenth Century European Books and Manuscripts
Nineteenth Century English Books and Manuscripts
Nineteenth Century American Books and Manuscripts
Twentieth Century European Books and Manuscripts
Twentieth Century English Books and Manuscripts
Twentieth Century American Books and Manuscripts

A unique feature of this report is that it omits references to funding, staff, exhibitions, publications, and everything else related to the functioning of a rare book collection.

But what of the private institution not attached to a university, a rare book library like the Newberry in Chicago? *The Annual Report of the Newberry Library for the Year Ending June 30, 1982* is a tribute to Lawrence W. Towner, its director, and his twenty years at the library. The Newberry's *Annual Report* is in a category by itself, more reminiscent of something produced by a large corporation than by a library. In addition to maintaining a collection of rare books and manuscripts, the Newberry also performs a variety of other activities, as witnessed in the Table of Contents of its forty-two-page *Annual Report* for 1981-1982:

From the Chairman of the Board of Trustees
From the President and Librarian
Acquisitions at the Newberry: Brittle Books Programs
The New Bookstack Building
Research and Education at the Newberry: The Family and Community History Center.
The Newberry Library Associates and Volunteers
Appendices:
  1. Trustees and Officers: Trustee Committees
  2. Staff of the Newberry Library
  3. Newberry Library Volunteers

4. Readers' Services
5. Acquisitions of Books and Library Materials
6. Newberry Library Publications
7. Scholarly Activities of Staff
8. Newberry Library Events
9. Newberry Library Fellows and Institute Participants
10. Donors of Signficant Gifts of Library Materials
11. Donors of Cash or Securities
12. The Campaign for the Newberry Library
13. Newberry Library Associates
14. Funds for Restricted Purposes
15. Financial Statements

It is rather surprising that, though the Newberry has added $15 million worth of acquisitions over the past twenty years[15] and spends a few hundred thousand dollars annually on further acquisitions, its annual report does not discuss its most recent acquisitions in more detail, as for instance Yale does. Two pages by James M. Wells, vice president and curator of rare books and manuscripts, discuss both the plan to replace brittle works, chiefly reference materials, and the names of the donors of a few acquisitions and the general subject of those acquisitions. For example—"Mrs. Dorothy G. Hedin gave 279 books published by Stone & Kimball and Herbert Stuart Stone and Company, many of them hitherto unrepresented in our large Stone & Kimball Collection,"[16] or "Mr. Andrew McNally III gave a collection of globes, maps, and astrolabes,"[17] or "Mrs. Edward Loewenthal gave a fifteenth century French Book of Hours, handsomely illuminated," (and here a photo is included), but he does not say what Stone & Kimball titles were given, nor anything distinctive about the globes and maps, and finally no bibliographical citation whatsoever was given about the "fifteenth century French Book of Hours." There is nothing more detailed than that in the report other than the total number of titles added (6,880) to the collection. This is where Yale shows the way. But as the library is generally divided into five separate acquisitional departments (the General Collection, the Edward E. Ayer Collection, the Everett D. Graff Collection, the Wm. B. Greenlee Collection, and the John M. Wing Collection), it is surprising that each of these collections does not receive at least one special page.

On the other hand, the Newberry Library, which contains some real gems for the rare book curator, does mention other things that not all other libraries do. It names every member of its staff and discusses

A reading room of the Newberry Library. Courtesy of the Newberry Library, Chicago.

their scholarly activities. It lists all of its latest publications and mentions the series of lectures, seminars, and other activities held at the Library during the year (e.g., "Chicago Colloquia on Latin American History," "Center for the History of the American Indian Seminars," "Center for Renaissance Studies Seminars and Lectures," "The Center for the History of the American Indian Fourth Annual Conference, the Metis in North America," and "The Newberry Library Renaissance Conference, Humanism and Schooling in Renaissance Europe." This is commendable and points out what a first rate rare book library should be able to sponsor but rarely does. But why is there no list of the library's exhibits?

The Newberry does provide some statistics on readers' services, acquisitions, cataloging, etc., which are worth pointing out, in order to illustrate their approach:[18]

## READERS' SERVICES

ADMISSIONS:  1980–81: 8,594   1981–82: 5,930*

### READER-DAYS

|  | July 1, 1980-<br>June 30, 1981 | July 1, 1981-<br>June 30, 1982 |
|---|---|---|
| Main Reading Room | 9,587 | 7,321 |
| Local and Family History | 11,141 | 7,081 |
| Special Collections | 6,868 | 5,401 |
| Resident Scholars | 15,779 | 11,010 |
|  | 43,376 | 30,813 |

### BOOKS PAGED

|  | July 1, 1980-<br>June 30, 1981 | July 1, 1981-<br>June 30, 1982 |
|---|---|---|
| Main Reading Room | 34,434 | 25,241 |
| Local and Family History | 79,459 | 54,544 |
| Special Collections | 27,913 | 22,272 |
| Total Books Paged | 141,806 | 102,057 |

The Newberry breaks down each collection in two ways, one listing the titles added to that collection by the year, and the other by books cataloged in each collection each year. This is the chart showing titles added:[9]

## ACQUISITIONS

TITLES ADDED TO THE COLLECTIONS

|  | July 1, 1980-<br>June 30, 1981 | July 1, 1981-<br>June 30, 1982 |
|---|---|---|

*Some of the facilities were closed for several months for construction and the moving of collections, thus the lower number of readers.

## GENERAL COLLECTION
Purchases
  General Funds

|  |  |  |
|---|---:|---:|
|  | 5,058 | 4,543 |
| Jane Oakley | 389 | 419 |
| Gifts | 433 | 733 |
|  | 5,880 | 5,695 |

## EDWARD E. AYER COLLECTION

|  |  |  |
|---|---:|---:|
| Purchases | 880 | 821 |
| Gifts | 27 | 29 |
|  | 907 | 850 |

## EDWARD D. GRAFF COLLECTION

|  |  |  |
|---|---:|---:|
| Purchases | 9 | 1 |
| Gifts | 2 | 3 |
|  | 11 | 4 |

## WILLIAM B. GREENLEE COLLECTION

|  |  |  |
|---|---:|---:|
| Purchases | 45 | 38 |
| Gifts | 0 | 0 |
|  | 45 | 38 |

## JOHN M. WING FOUNDATION COLLECTION

|  |  |  |
|---|---:|---:|
| Purchases | 340 | 195 |
|  | 55 | 98 |
|  | 395 | 293 |
| TOTAL | 7,238 | 6,880 |

Under Cataloging there is an additional group entitled "Other" which includes microcards, microfiche, microfilm, recataloging, and withdrawn.

Appendix 9 of the Newberry Report provides an impressive list of Fellows working in the various collections, and they include some of the following categories: National Endowment for the Humanities Fellows (5), Monticello College Foundation Fellow (1), Exxon Education Foundation Fellows (3), Newberry British Academy Exchange Fellows (2),

Newberry Library Fellows (14), Newberry Library Associate Fellows (11), Center for the History of the American Indian Fellows (3), D'Arcy McNickle Memorial Fellows (8), Center for Renaissance Studies Fellows (5), etc. It is an impressive list of researchers (and endowments).

Raising funds and attracting gifts for a private library such as the Newberry is naturally big business, and it is not surprising, therefore, that donors are given considerable recognition in the *Annual Report*. A donor of as little as $25 may have his or her name printed in the report. In fact, donors are listed in the following categories:

Donors of Significant Gifts of Library Materials

Donors of Cash, or Securities (including corporation, estates, foundations, and trusts, donors of cash, securities, or property)

The Campaign for the Newberry Library: To Preserve These Uncommon Collections

Newberry Library Associates (includes: "Benefactors," donating $500 or more, "Sustaining Associates," donating $300 or more, "Patrons," donating $200 or more, "Contributing Associates," for amounts of $100 or more, "Associates," for $50 or more, and "Junior Associates," for donations of $25 or more.

The Newberry's endowment and funding programs have become so successful that donations ($3,333,524) exceeded Dividends and Interest Income (of $2,377,651). Compare these figures with those of Yale (1980-81) in Figure 1. Different libraries emphasize different aspects of their holdings. The Hillman Library at the University of Pittsburgh is typical of a library where special collections play a fairly small role.

Heretofore special collections at Pittsburgh did not have its own budget, and even now the department runs on under $20,000 a year, so that the *Annual Report* of the Hillman Library's Special Collections Department (exclusive of Archives) is rather impressive. The report prepared for July 1981-June 1982 by Charles E. Aston, Jr., was divided into the following categories:

Public Service
Special Reference
Exhibits and Special Events
Acquisitions
Cataloging and Processing
Conservation and Preservation

The Collections
  Archive of Popular Culture
  Curtis Theatre Collection
  Darlington Memorial Library
  Rudolf Carnap Collection
  Personnel and Staff Activities

Through the careful collection of statistics, the curator was able to provide the details of every user of every collection (and distinguish his or her rank—faculty, graduate, undergraduate, alumnus, visitor), the total number of volumes paged in each collection, and the number of periodicals and manuscript pieces requested.

Expenses, however, were broken down in the most rudimentary fashion.

Special Collection Monographs: Bibliography & Reference,
  Small Press Poetry, Fine Printing, 19th Century Imprints,
  Wittgenstein Papers (film)
Standing Order/Continuations
Subscriptions
Binding
Total Materials expense

But of course there were no endowment funds or significant gifts from which to draw.

Cataloging statistics were provided in a series of charts—which also included usage—as in the following example:[20]

## SPECIAL COLLECTIONS CATALOGING STATISTICS
## REPORT FOR 1980/81

| Catalogued in Special Collections | Special Coll. | Curtis | Darlington | Total |
|---|---|---|---|---|
| Original | 181 | 8 | 0 | 189 |
| Library of Congress | 75 | 5 | 0 | 80 |
| Added Volumes | 367 | 0 | 0 | 367 |
| Total Volumes | 625 | 13 | 0 | 636 |
| Recatalogued | 7 | 1 | 0 | 8 |
| Reclassed | 14 | 0 | 0 | 14 |
| Analytics | 11 | 0 | 0 | 11 |

As the Hillman Library had just trained its first conservator, no figures were available on conservation and preservation.

There is much to consider when the curator of a special collections department drafts an annual report. Through a fairly representative variety of annual reports from libraries across the country, we have seen how emphasis may change: In scientifically-minded Minnesota, it is data and quantities that count; at Yale, where the humanists still prevail, the emphasis is on the significance of each important acquisition. But there are certain basic categories that a curator should try to apply and to modify as needed. A model annual report might include the following:

The Annual Report of the Special Collections Department

*Introduction*

This could discuss any major changes, or events of special importance, including trends in the use of the library. Was it a good year or a bad one, and why?

*Acquisitions*

A narrative discussion of gifts and purchases of books, manuscripts, maps, etc., should be presented, preferably in the Yale model. Stress the significance of each major new item, how it was acquired, by whom, and through which fund.

*The Collections*

Each of the collections should be discussed separately, explaining how each may have developed towards meeting projected goals of the Acquisition Policy. What are the immediate aims? How many materials were used in each, and by whom? Provide statistics.

*Exhibitions*

Name and list each exhibition, times, locations, attendance, lectures, significance. Provide good photographs of choice displays and lectures. Include a copy of the program or brochure for each one.

*Other Special Events*

Special courses, seminars, or even public lectures. Acquisition of a famous rare book library or works. Special receptions for visiting dignitaries or for exhibitions before opened to public.

*Publications*

To publish special catalogs of your holdings (as do Newberry, Harvard, or Yale), to publish the letters of special individuals (as Yale has done for the Horace Walpole papers), or even to publish detailed catalogs of special exhibitions held.

*Projects*

These may be in partial execution of the goals established in your Acquisition Policy, or they may be to add holdings to OCLC, etc.; to make a conservation/preservation study; to consider adding a new collection and its effects on the budget; to add a new wing to the building; to start a new endowment fund; to microfilm brittle works, etc.

*Use of Collections*

As this would determine the use of each collection, by whom, subjects studied, number of materials used, etc., this category might just as easily be incorporated under the previous rubric, "The Collections," or else in a statistical appendix.

*Conservation-Preservation*

This could be a statistical analysis of what has been accomplished in the binding, repairs, preservation, etc., e.g., as was seen on page 139 for the categories by Yale: Conservation (books, protective cases, paper), Binding (pamphlets, volumes rebound), Repairs (volumes, inserts, etc.).

*Fellowships*

This admittedly will apply only to the larger, well-endowed institutions, such as the Hoover Institution, Yale, Harvard, or the Newberry. The recipients, their awards, the titles of their works, and their publications can be published annually even in a separate volume, as the American Philosophical Society does.

*Gifts and Donations*

List names of donors—whether corporations, foundations, or individuals. Both Yale and the Newberry handle the matter expertly. There should be a separate list for the total new annual endowments each year.

*Media Coverage*

Collect all articles in newspapers and journals on your institution. If films have been made, or special television coverage, document this.

*Staff and Their Activities*

List all staff members and their ranks, degrees, assigned jobs, and any special achievements. Let them know they are appreciated. If they write articles or give lectures, acknowledge this.

*Comparative Financial Data*

Prepare very detailed budgets, and compare these figures with preceding years. Something similar to the data provided by Rogers in Figure 1 would be appropriate.

*Statistical Appendixes*

What is included here depends upon the extent to which the curator has already used these figures elsewhere in the annual report, but this would be a natural place for figures on circulation or cataloging.

## References

1. Henry E. Huntington Library and Art Gallery. *Annual Report, July 1, 1970–June 30, 1971.* San Marino, Calif.
2. *Report of the University Librarian, July 1980-June 1981.* Special issue, January 1982, *Bulletin of Yale University,* pp. 23-25.
3. *Ibid.,* p. 25.
4. *Ibid.,* p. 27.
5. *Ibid.*
6. *Ibid.,* p. 30.
7. *Ibid.*
8. *Ibid.,* p. 37.
9. *Ibid.,* p. 42.
10. *Ibid.,* p. 57.
11. *Ibid.,* pp. 58-59.
12. *Ibid.,* p. 59.
13. *Ibid.,* p. 61.
14. *The Houghton Library Report of Accessions for the Year.* Harvard College Library, Cambridge, Mass., 1965.
15. *The Newberry Library Annual Report, July 1, 1981-June 30, 1982* (Chicago: Newberry Library, 1982), p. 2.
16. *Ibid.,* p. 5.
17. *Ibid.*
18. *Ibid.,* pp. 15–16.
19. *Ibid.,* p. 15.
20. *Annual Report, Special Collections Department, University of Pittsburgh Libraries, July 1980–June 1981.* August 1981.

# 9

# Organizations and Libraries

There are various organizations and societies which the curator of special collections may wish to join or consult, and these are listed in the first section of this chapter. Naturally, there are a good many additional organizations for the specialist interested in anything from psychology to paper making. Apart from a few formal societies concerned specifically with rare books and manuscripts, the curator of special collections must assess the particular concerns of his or her collection and may also wish to contact professors and other scholars in a specialized field. Most professors and societies are quite helpful, and the personal contacts established may prove especially valuable over the years.

The second section of this chapter contains a list of some of the national libraries throughout Europe and the rest of the world, which may serve as useful references. The final section contains a list of networks and their affiliates in this country.

## PROFESSIONAL ORGANIZATIONS

AFRICAN STUDIES ASSOCIATION
255 Kinsey Hall
405 Hilgard Ave.
University of California
Los Angeles, CA 90024

This society was founded in 1957 and has over two thousand members. Its stated purpose: "To facilitate communication and to stimulate research among scholars." The Association is interested in anything to do with African history, political science, geography, etc. It publishes the *African Studies Review* on a quarterly basis, as well as bibliographical material.

ALCUIN SOCIETY
Box 94108
Richmond, British Columbia V6Y 2H2
Canada

Founded in 1965, this small society (of about 350 members) is concerned with book collecting and fine limited editions. It publishes its own quarterly, *Amphora.*

THE AMERICAN ANTIQUARIAN SOCIETY
185 Salisbury St.
Worcester, MA 01609

The Society has some eight hundred members and publishes its annual *Proceedings.*

AMERICAN ASSOCIATION OF MUSEUMS
1055 Thomas Jefferson St., N.W.
Washington, DC 20007

This large organization (7,000 members) was founded in 1906 and now has a permanent staff of thirty. It includes all types of museums and librarians and curators of those museums. It publishes a monthly newsletter, *Aviso,* and the bimonthly *Museum News,* as well as an official annual directory of museums. It also publishes some books on such special topics as fine arts insurance and sponsors some training courses.

AMERICAN ASSOCIATION FOR STATE AND LOCAL HISTORY (formerly Council of Historical Societies)
708 Berry Rd.
Nashville, TN 37204

Founded in 1940, the 7,500 members publish several useful books on archives and preservation and conduct seminars and workshops.

AMERICAN CATHOLIC HISTORICAL ASSOCIATION
Catholic University of America
Washington, DC 20064

Founded in 1919, this society is chiefly interested in the history of the Catholic church both in the U.S. and abroad.

AMERICAN HISTORICAL ASSOCIATION
400 A St., S.E.
Washington, DC 20003

One of the oldest historical organizations in this country (founded in 1884), and by far the largest with nearly 15,000 members, the Association serves as a vast umbrella for numerous affiliated historical societies on almost every aspect of American and world history. It offers many prizes and services and publishes the *American Historical Review* quarterly, which includes articles, book reviews (on books in numerous languages), and bibliographical information. For the historical curator, questions directed to the executive director should result in answers. In addition, the AHA has one massive national convention per year, with a full schedule of papers read on a variety of subjects.

## AMERICAN LIBRARY ASSOCIATION
50 E. Huron St.
Chicago, IL 60611

This is the largest (37,000 members) and oldest (1876) such society in the United States, with a stated mission: "To promote and improve library service and librarianship, establish standards of service, promote the recruiting of personnel." The ALA is composed of a number of active committees, e.g., Accreditation; Intellectual Freedom; International Relations; Mediation, Arbitration and Inquiry; Library Administration; Legislation, and has a sub-unit especially interested in rare books and manuscripts. Divided into fifty-six regional groups, the ALA publishes *Booklist, American Libraries,* and a variety of monographs and pamphlets.

## AMERICAN SOCIETY OF BOOKPLATE COLLECTORS AND DESIGNERS
1206 N. Stoneman Ave., No. 15
Alhambra, CA 91801

The ASBCD was founded in 1922 and has 250 members—collectors, designers, engravers, etc.—and publishes *Bookplates in the News* and a yearbook.

## AMERICAN SOCIETY FOR EIGHTEENTH-CENTURY STUDIES
421 Denney Hall
Ohio State University
Columbus, OH 43210

This society was founded in 1969, has about two thousand members, and is interested in English and American 18th century history, literature, and fine arts. They publish a quarterly, *Eighteenth-Century Studies.*

ARCHONS OF COLOPHON
c/o *Encyclopedia of Associations*
Gale Research Co.
Book Tower
Detroit, MI 48226

This unique society was founded in 1909 and consists of 182 members who hold high administrative or teaching posts. Membership is by invitation only.

ASOCIACIÓN MEXICANA DE BIBLIOTECARIOS
Apartado Postal 127-132
México 7, D.F.

ASOCIACIÓN NACIONAL DE BIBLIOTECARIOS, ARCHIVAROS Y ARQUEOLOGOS
Avenida de Calvo Sotel 22
Apartado Postal 14281
Madrid, Spain

ASSOCIACAO PORTUGUESA DE BIBLIOTECARIAS, ARQUIVISTAS E DOCUMENTALISTA
Edificio da Biblioteca Nacional
Campo Grande 83
1700 Lisbon
Portugal

ASSOCIATION BELGE DE DOCUMENTATION
Rue Joseph Schols, 62
B-1080 Brussels
Belgium

ASSOCIATION DES ARCHIVISTES FRANÇAIS
60 rue des Francs-Bourgeois
75141 Paris Cedex 03
France

ASSOCIATION DES BIBLIOTHÉCAIRES DE FRANCE
65 rue de Richelieu
75002 Paris Cedex 02
France

ASSOCIATION FOR ASIAN STUDIES
One Lane Hall
University of Michigan
Ann Arbor, MI 48109

Founded in 1941, with over five thousand members, this active association is interested in many countries and aspects of their literature, history, politics, etc., and has numerous committees, e.g., Southeast Asia Research Materials; Asian Law; East Asian Libraries, etc. It publishes a *Newsletter,* the *Journal of Asian Studies, Bibliography of Asian Studies,* and occasional monographs.

ASSOCIATION FOR THE BIBLIOGRAPHY OF HISTORY
Department of History
Georgia State University
Atlanta, GA 30303

This society of 200 historians, bibliographers, and librarians was founded in 1978 to promote development of bibliographical skills.

ASSOCIATION OF ANCIENT HISTORIANS
Department of Classics
University of British Columbia
Vancouver, British Columbia
Canada V6T 1W5

This small society was founded in 1974 and concentrates on classical history.

ASSOCIATION OF COLLEGE AND RESEARCH LIBRARIES (ACRL)
50 E. Huron St.
Chicago, IL 60611

Founded in 1889, ACRL now has nearly ten thousand members. It was founded in order to promote the profession and career development in academic and research libraries. This society has a special section, "Rare Books and Manuscripts," as a sub-unit of the association. It publishes College and Research Libraries *News* and a bi-monthly, *College and Research Libraries.*

ASSOCIATION OF RESEARCH LIBRARIES
1527 New Hampshire Ave., N.W.
Washington, DC 20036

This organization publishes newsletters, *Salary Survey, Statistics Annual,* and associated with this is the Office of Management Studies, which publishes the *SPEC Flyers* and *Kits* referred to in this book. Founded in 1970, the Association has a few publications on conservation and collection analysis and has produced some valuable surveys.

ASSOCIAZONE ITALIANA BIBLIOTECHE
Istituto di Patologia del Libro
Via Milano 76
00184 Rome
Italy

AUSTRALIAN SOCIETY OF ARCHIVISTS
c/o Library Association of Australia
Box M222
Sydney Mail Exchange, New South Wales 2012
Australia

This society publishes *Archives and Manuscripts.*

BIBLIOGRAPHICAL SOCIETY
c/o *Library*
Oxford University Press
Walton St.
Oxford OX2 6DP
England

BIBLIOGRAPHICAL SOCIETY OF AMERICA
Box 397
Grand Central Station
New York, NY 10017

Founded in 1904, it now has over 1,400 members, chiefly collectors and curators.

BIBLIOGRAPHICAL SOCIETY OF CANADA
Box 1878
Guelph, Ontario N1H 7A1
Canada

BINDERS' GUILD
Route 3, Box 289
Zebulon, NC 27597

Founded in 1977 by forty members, it is chiefly interested in amateur and professional hand bookbinding.

## THE BOSTONIAN SOCIETY
Old State House
206 Washington St.
Boston, MA 02109

Founded in 1881, with over 1,300 members, it has a choice library of 12,000 volumes and manuscripts on the history of Boston. It publishes its *Proceedings.*

## THE BRITISH RECORDS ASSOCIATION
Master's Court
The Charterhouse
Charterhouse Square
London, EC1M 6AU 1949, U.K.

This society publishes *Archives.*

## THE CANADIAN HISTORICAL ASSOCIATION
c/o Public Archives of Canada
395 Wellington St.
Ottawa, Ontario K1A ON3
Canada

Publishes a newsletter.

## THE CANADIAN LIBRARY ASSOCIATION
151 Sparks St.
Ottawa, Ontario K1P 5E3
Canada

## EARLY ENGLISH TEXT SOCIETY
Lady Margaret Hall
Oxford, England

Founded in 1864, this society of international scholars has a membership of over 1,200. It publishes pre-1558 texts not otherwise available, e.g., works such as Beowulf, those of King Alfred, Piers Plowman, and medieval drama.

## GROLIER CLUB
47 E. 60th St.
New York, NY 10022

With a membership of 655, this club dates back to 1884 and has a private library of 65,000 volumes. It publishes a yearbook, a gazette, and some books.

HAKLUYT SOCIETY
c/o Map Library
The British Library
Great Russell St.
London, WC1B 3DG
England

This society, founded in 1846 and with over two thousand members, is especially interested in the literature of travel, geography, voyages, and expeditions. It has an annual meeting in London and has published over 300 titles, including reprints of original texts.

THE HISPANIC SOCIETY OF AMERICA
613 W. 155th St.
New York, NY 10032

Dating back to 1904, this society, which numbers four hundred members, has a research institute which maintains a museum of paintings and sculpture, in addition to a library of 200,000 manuscripts and 15,000 books printed before 1701 (including 250 incunabula), and another 150,000 books on Spain, Portugal, and colonial Hispanic America. The Society also publishes books occasionally.

INDIAN LIBRARY ASSOCIATION
A/40-41 Flat No. 201
Ansal Buildings
Delhi
110009 India

INTERNATIONAL AFRICAN INSTITUTE
38 King St.
London WC2E 8JR
England

This institute was founded in 1926 and has some two thousand members. Its "primary aim is to promote the serious study of African peoples." It publishes the quarterly, *Africa,* and monographs on linguistics, etc.

LIBRARY ASSOCIATION
7 Ridgmont St.
London WC1E 7AE, U.K.

It publishes the *Record*.

THE LIBRARY ASSOCIATON
Rare Books Group
c/o Miss J. Archibald
British Library
Great Russell St.
London WC1B 3DG, U.K.

It has a membership of 1,250 and publishes a newsletter.

THE MEDIEVAL ACADEMY OF AMERICA
1420 Massachusetts Ave.
Cambridge, MA 02138

Although it was founded in 1925 and has a membership of over 4,000, this society is not well known to the public at large, though most research libraries carry its quarterly review, *Speculum*. The Academy has also published ninety books on the medieval period, covering the period from A.D. 500–1500. It promotes research, publication, and instruction in medieval records, art, archaeology, history, law, etc.

MODERN LANGUAGE ASSOCIATION OF AMERICA
10 Astor Pl.
New York, NY 10003

This well-known society dates back to 1883 and has some 28,000 members. It is affiliated with the Association of Departments of English and the Association of Departments of Foreign Languages, and is interested in university scholarship in the fields of English and modern foreign languages. It is currently developing a computerized bibliographic system encompassing the entire field of literature and linguistics. It publishes a newsletter, the quarterly journal, *PMLA,* and an *International Bibliography*.

THE NATIONAL TRUST FOR HISTORIC PRESERVATION
1785 Massachusetts Ave., N.W.
Washington, DC 20036

Founded in 1949, the NTHP's membership already exceeds 130,000. In addition to its 10,000-volume library on historic preservation, it publishes *Historic Preservation* and gives seminars and workshops on the preservation of historic sites.

ORGANIZATION OF AMERICAN HISTORIANS
112 N. Bryan St.
Bloomington, IN 47401

12,500 members established the society in 1907 and have created committees on archives, historic preservation, etc. The OAH publishes the *Journal of American History.*

## PRIVATE LIBRARIES ASSOCIATION
Ravelston
South View Road
Pinner, Middlesex, U.K.

With a membership of 1,200, the Association was established in 1957 by rare book collectors to encourage cooperation among book collectors generally, and sponsors the Society of Private Printers and the Bookplate Club. It publishes two quarterlies, *Exchange List* and the *Private Library,* as well as an annual, *Private Press Books.*

## RENAISSANCE ENGLISH TEXT SOCIETY
c/o James M. Wells
Newberry Libray
60 W. Walton St.
Chicago, IL 60610

This society was established in 1959 to publish scarce literary texts, chiefly non-dramatic works produced during the period 1475-1660.

## SOCIETY FOR FRENCH HISTORICAL STUDIES
c/o Dr. Alexander Sedgewick
Department of History
Randall Hall
University of Virginia
Charlottesville, VA 22903

Founded in 1955, its nearly 1,500 members are professional historians who sponsor an annual convention and publish *French Historical Studies,* the most important journal on French history published in this country.

## SOCIETY FOR ITALIAN HISTORICAL STUDIES
Boston College
c/o Dr. Alan J. Reinerman
Chestnut Hill, MA 02167

## SOCIETY FOR THE PROMOTION OF HELLENIC STUDIES
31-34 Gordon Square
London, WC1H OPP, U.K.

Its 2,800 members are chiefly academics in the classics and archaeology. Founded in 1880, the Society maintains a 50,000 volume library, sponsors lectures, and publishes the *Journal of Hellenic Studies.*

## SOCIETY OF AMERICAN HISTORIANS
610 Fayerweather Hall
Columbia University
New York, NY 10027

The Society was founded in 1939. Its membership is by invitation only, limited to 250 scholars have written at least one book on American history.

## SOCIETY OF AMERICAN ARCHIVISTS
330 S. Wells St., Suite 810
Chicago, IL 60606

This society was founded in 1931 and has four thousand members. It maintians sub-units of special interests: College and University Archives, Manuscript Collections, Description of Records and Manuscripts, etc. The Society publishes the *American Archivist.*

## TYPOPHILES
140 Lincoln Road
Brooklyn, NY 11225

This society of 500 members was founded in 1930 and is composed of designers, printers, book collectors, private press owners, etc.

## VEREIN DEUTSCHER BIBLIOTHEKARE
Frauenlobstrasse 22
6000 Frankfurt 90
West Germany

## WESTERN ASSOCIATION OF MAP LIBRARIANS
c/o Stanley D. Stevens
Map Librarian
University of California
The Library
Santa Cruz, CA 95064

This small society was founded in 1967.

## NATIONAL LIBRARIES

ANG PAMBANSANG AKLAN
(The National Library)
T. M. Kalaw
Ermita
Manila, The Philippines

ARCHIVOS HISTÓRICOS Y BIBLIOTECAS
Instituto Nacional de Antropología e Historia
Calzada M. Gandhi y Paseo de la Reforma
México 5, D.F.

BIBLIOTECA APOSTOLICA VATICANA
00120 Cittá del Vaticana
Vatican City

BIBLIOTECA CENTRALĂ DE STAT A REPUBLICI SÓCIALISTE
Bucharest
Str. Jon Ghica nr. 4
Romania

BIBLIOTECA NACIONAL
Calle México 564
Buenos Aires
Argentina

BIBLIOTECA NACIONAL
Av. Rio Branco
219-31-2C-21
Rio de Janeiro GB
Brazil

BIBLIOTECA NACIONAL
Avenida Bernardo O'Higgins 651
Santiago, Chile

BIBLIOTECA NACIONAL
Rua Ocidental do Campo Grande 83
1700 Lisbon
Portugal

BIBLIOTECA NACIONAL
Calvo Sotelo 20
Madrid 1
Spain

BIBLIOTECA NACIONAL
Apartado 6525
Caracas 101
Venezuela

BIBLIOTECA NAZIONALE CENTRALE
Piazza Cavalleggeri
Florence, Italy

BIBLIOTEKA UNIWERSYTEKA w WARSZAWIE
Krakowskia Przedmieście 26/28
Warsaw
Poland

BIBLIOTHÈQUE NATIONALE
58 rue de Richelieu
75084 Paris Cedex 02
France

BIBLIOTHÈQUE NATIONALE D'ALGÉRIE
1 avenue de Dr Franz Fanon
Algiers
Algeria

BIBLIOTHÈQUE NATIONALE DU GRAND-DUCHÉ
DE LUXEMBOURG
37 Boulevard F. D. Roosevelt
Luxembourg

BIBLIOTHÈQUE ROYAL ALBERT 1er
Boulevard de l'Empereur 4
B-1000 Brussels
Belgium

BODLEIAN LIBRARY
Oxford University
Oxford OX1 3B6
England

THE BRITISH LIBRARY
Great Russell St.
London WC1B 3DG
England

DET KONELIGE BIBLIOTEK
Christians Brygge 8
DK-1219 Copenhagen
Denmark

DEUTSCHE STAATSBIBLIOTHEK
DDR-108 Berlin
Unter den Linden 8
Postfach 1312
German Democratic Republic (East Germany)

THE EGYPTIAN NATIONAL LIBRARY
General Egyptian Book Organization
Nile Corniche
Boulac
Cairo, Egypt

GOSUDARSTVENNAYA ORDENA LENINA BIBLIOTEKA SSR IMENI
V.I. LENINA
(Lenin State Library)
Moscow
Tsentr, pr. Kalinina 3
U.S.S.R.

INSTITUTO NACIONAL DE CULTURA
Biblioteca Nacional
Apartado Postal 2335
Lima, Peru

JEWISH NATIONAL AND UNIVERSITY LIBRARY
Box 503
Jerusalem, Israel

KONINKLIJKE BIBLIOTHEEK
Lange Voorhout 34
Den Haag
The Netherlands

KUNGLIGA BIBLIOTEKET
Box 5039
S-10241 Stockholm 5
Sweden

LIBRARY OF CONGRESS
Washington, DC 20540

MILLÎ KÜTÜPHANE GENEL MÜDÜRLÜGÜ (National Library)
Kumrular Sokak
Kizilay
Ankara, Turkey

NARODNA BIBLIOTEKA SOCIJALISTĬCKE REPUBLIKE SRBIJE
11000 Belgrade
Skerlićeva 1
Yugoslavia

NATIONAL CENTRAL LIBRARY
43 Nan Hai Road
Taipei
Taiwan

NATIONAL LIBRARY
44 The Terrace
Wellington
Box 8016
New Zealand

NATIONAL LIBRARY
Stamford Rd.
Singapore 6

NATIONAL LIBRARY OF AUSTRALIA
Parkes Place
Canberra ACT 2600
Australia

NATIONAL LIBRARY OF CANADA
395 Wellington St.
Ottawa, Ontario K1A ON4
Canada

NATIONAL LIBRARY OF GREECE
Panepistemiou St.
Athens, Greece

NATIONAL LIBRARY OF INDIA
Belvedere
Calcutta 27
India

NATIONAL LIBRARY OF IRELAND
Kildare St.
Dublin 2
Republic of Ireland

NATIONAL LIBRARY OF SCOTLAND
George IV Bridge
Edinburgh EH1 1EW
Scotland

NATIONAL LIBRARY OF THAILAND
Samsen Road
Bangkok 3
Thailand

OSTERREICHISCHE NATIONALBIBLIOTHEK
Josefsplatz 1
A-1014 Vienna
Austria

ORSZÁGOS SZÉCHÉNYI KÖNYVTÁR [National Library]
H-1827 Budapest
Muzeum Krt. 14–16
Hungary

PEI-CHING T'U SHU KUAN [National Library of China]
Peking 7
China

PUBLIC ARCHIVES OF CANADA
395 Wellington St.
Ottawa, Ontario K1A ON3
Canada

SCHWEIZERISCHE LANDESBIBLIOTHEK
Hallwylstraße 15
CH-3003 Bern
Switzerland

STAASBIBLIOTHEK PREUSSISCHER KULTURBESITZ
D-1 Berlin 30 (Tiergarten)
Potsdamer Straße 33
Postfach 1407
Federal Republic of Germany (West Germany)

STATE LIBRARY
Box 397
239 Vermeulen St.
Pretoria 0001
South Africa

STÁTNÍ KNIKNOVRA ČESKÉ SOCIALISTICKÉ REPUBLIKY
[State Library]
Klementinum 190
110 01 Prague 1
Czechoslovakia

THU VIỆN QUOC GIA VIET NAM
[National Library]
31 Tràng Thi
Hanoi
Democratic Republic of Viet Nam

UNIVERSITETS BIBLIOTEKET I OSLO
[Royal University Library]
Drammensveien
Oslo 2, Norway

UNIVERSITY OF TOKYO LIBRARY
3-1 Hongo 7-chome
Bunkyo-Ku
Tokyo 113, Japan
(Japan has no national library.)

## NETWORKS AND AFFILIATES

AMIGOS—Bibliographic Council
11300 N. Central Expressway
Suite 321
Dallas, TX 75243

BCR—Bibliographical Center for Research, Rocky Mountain Region, Inc.
245 Columbine
Suite 212
Denver, CO 80206

CLASS—California Library Author for Systems and Services
1415 Koll Circle
Suite 101
San Jose, CA 95112

CAPCON—Capital Consortium Network
1717 Massachusetts Ave., N.W.
Washington, DC 20036

CCLC—Cooperative College Library Center
159 Forrest Ave., N.E.
Suite 602
Atlanta, GA 30308

FEDLINK—The Federal Library and Information Network
Federal Library Committee
Library of Congress
Navy Yard Annex, Room 400
Washington, DC 20540

FEDLINK provides services to various federal libraries as well as to OCLC,
Inc., BRS, etc.

FAUL—Five Associated University Libraries
757 Ostrom Ave.
Syracuse, NY 13210

ILLINET—The Illinois Library and Information Network
Illinois State Library
Centennial Building
Springfield, IL 62756

INCOLSA—Indiana Cooperative Library Services Authority
1100 W. 42nd St.
Indianapolis, IN 46208

MLC—Michigan Library Consortium
720 Science Library
Wayne State University
Detroit, MI 48202

MIDLNET—Midwest Regional Library Network
c/o University of Wisconsin-Green Bay
Green Bay, WI 54302

MINITEX—Minnesota Interlibrary Telecommunications Exchange
University of Minnesota
30 Wilson Library
Minneapolis, MN 55455

NELINET—New England Library Information Network
385 Elliot St.
Newton, MA 02164

OCLC, Inc.
6565 Frantz Road
Dublin, OH 43017–0702

OHIONET
2929 Kenny Road
Suite 280
Columbus, OH 43221

PALINET
3420 Walnut St.
Philadelphia, PA 19104

PRLC—Pittsburgh Regional Library Center
Chatham College
100 Woodland Road
Pittsburgh, PA 15232

RLG—Research Libraries Group, Inc.
Jordan Quadrangle
Stanford, CA 94305
Responsible for RLIN.

SOLINET—Southeastern Library Network, Inc.
615 Peachtree St., N.E.
Suite 410
Atlanta, GA 30308

SUNY/OCLC
SUNY Plaza
Albany, NY 12246
(This is one of the 20 OCLC, Inc., affiliated networks.)

UTLAS—University of Toronto Library Automation System
130 St. George St.
Toronto, Ontario
Canada, M5S 1A5

WLN—Washington Library Network
Washington State Library
Olympia, WA 98504

WLC—Wisconsin Library Consortium
University of Wisconsin
464 Memorial Library
728 State St.
Madison, WI 53706

# 10

# Reference Works

The works included in this chapter are suggestions for the nucleus of a departmental reference section. Each category contains samples of the works currently available on each topic.

## BIBLIOGRAPHIC MANUALS AND ESSAYS

Barberi, Francesco, Panella, Antonio, et al. *Notizie Introduttive e Sussidi Bibliografici*. 3ª editzione rifatta ed accresciutta. Milano: Carlo Marzorati, 1958.
    This is an essential work for any library. The first volume deals with bibliographical problems in general, while the second concentrates entirely on Italian literature. Both volumes contain useful bibliographical references following each chapter.

*Bibliographic Description of Rare Books. Rules Formulated under AACR 2 and ISBD(A) for the Descriptive Cataloguing of Rare Books and Other Special Printed Materials*. Washington, D.C.: Library of Congress.

Binns, Norman E. *Introduction to Historical Bibliography*. London: Association of Assistant Librarians, 1953.

Blum, A. *Bibliographia. An Inquiry into Its Definition and Designations*. Trans. M.V. Rovelstad. Folkestone, Kent: Dawson—American Library Association, 1980.
    A critical historical study of bibliographical development. Excellent.

171

Bowers, Fredson T. *Principles of Bibliographical Description.* New York: Russell & Russell, 1962. A reprint of the 1949 Princeton edition. A basic work.

Gaskell, Philip. *A New Introduction to Bibliography.* Oxford: Clarendon Press, 1972.
Basic to any collection.

Gregg, Walter Wilson. *Collected Papers.* Oxford: Clarendon Press, 1966.

Haebler, Konrad. *The Study of Incunabula.* Trans. Lucy E. Osborne, with a Foreword by A.W. Pollard. New York: Grolier Club, 1933, reprinted by Kraus in 1967.
Comprises an elementary study of the critical bibliography of incunabula.

Maclès, Louise-Noëlle. *Manuel de Bibliographie.* 2ème édition. Paris: Presses Universitaires de France, 1969.
Typical of the excellence expected from French bibliographers, this work deals with bibliographies published throughout the world and is clearly stated, but is not a manual so much as a guide.

McCoum, Blanche P., and Jones, Helen D. *Bibliographical Procedures & Style. A Manual for Bibliographers in the Library of Congress.* Washington, D.C.: Library of Congress, 1966.

McKerrow, Ronald Brunless, ed. *An Introduction to Bibliography for Literary Students.* Oxford: Clarendon Press, 1962.

Padwick, Eric W. *Bibliographical Method. An Introductory Survey.* Cambridge & London: James Clarke & Co. 1969.

Pollard, Alfred W. "The Object and Methods of Bibliographical Collections and Descriptions," *The Library,* 2nd Series, VIII (1907), pp. 193–217.

Pollard, Alfred W., and Gregg, Walter Wilson. "Some Points in Bibliographical Description," *Transactions of the Bibliographical Society,* IX (1908), pp. 31–52.

Stokes, Roy. *Esdaile's Manual of Bibliography.* 5th rev. ed. Metuchen, N.J.: The Scarecrow Press, 1981.

Stokes, Roy. *The Function of Bibliography.* London: André Deutsch, 1969.

Van Hoesen, Henry B., and Walter, Frank K. *Bibliography, Practical Enumerative, Historical—An Introductory Manual.* New York: Charles Scribner's Sons, 1928.
Still a useful work with a large bibliographical index.

## BIBLIOGRAPHIES

### Americana

*The American Catalogue, July 1, 1876–December 31, 1910.* 21v. in 15.
New York: P. Smith, 1941 (reprint).
Contains the American national trade bibliography by "author-and-title alphabet," and by "subject alphabet."

*American Imprints, Historical Records Survey.* These were printed unevenly by some states, over unequal chronological periods.

Blanck, Jacob. *Bibliography of American Literature.* New Haven: Yale University Press, 1955-
Arranged alphabetically by author.

Brussel, Isidore R. *Anglo-American First Editions 1826–1900. East to West.* New York: R. R. Bowker, 1935.

Brussel, Isidore R. *Anglo-American First Editions 1826–1900. Part Two: West to East, 1786–1930.* New York: R. R. Bowker, 1936.

Evans, Charles. *American Bibliography: A Chronological Dictionary of All Books, Pamphlets and Periodical Articles Printed in the United States of America from the Genesis of Printing in 1639 down to and Including the Year 1800; with Bibliographical and Biographical Notes.* 12v. Chicago: Printed for the Author, 1903–1934.
A most valuable work, but listed chronologically, whereas J. Sabin listed by author, alphabetically.

Kelley, James. *American Catalogue of Books Published in the United States from January 1861 to January 1871.* 2v. 1866–1871.

Roorbach, Orville August. *Bibliotheca Americana. Catalogue of American Publications, Including Reprints and Original Works, from 1820 to 1852, Inclusive. Together with a List of Periodicals Published in the United States.* New York: P. Smith, 1939. (Reprint of the 1849 edition.)

Roorbach, Orville August. *Supplement to the Bibliotheca Americana. A Catalogue of American Publications, (Reprint and Original Works) from October, 1852, to May, 1855, Including Also a Repetition of such Books as have either Changed Prices or Publishers during that Period.* New York: P. Smith, 1939.

Roorbach, Orville August. *Addenda to the Bibliotheca Americana. A Catalogue of American Publications (Reprints and Original Works) from May, 1855, to March, 1858.* New York: P. Smith, 1939.

Roorbach, Orville August. *Volume IV. of the Bibliotheca Americana. A Catalogue of American Publications (Reprints and Original Works) from March, 1858, to January, 1861.* New York: P. Smith, 1939.
Roorbach also published numerous other "catalogues" on history, science, law, books, plays, etc., and also wrote books on horses and flowers.

Sabin, Joseph. *Bibliotheca Americana. Dictionary of Books Relating to America from Its Discovery to the Present Time.* 29v. New York: Bibliographical Society of America.
This excellent work is arranged by author.

### British, Irish, and European

Aldis, Harry Gidney. *A List of Books Printed in Scotland Before 1700.* Edinburgh: The Edinburgh Bibliographical Society, 1901.

Avanzi, Giannetto. *La Bibliografia Italiana (1921–46).* IIed. 5v. Roma: Istituto Nazionale per le Relazioni Culturali con l'Estero, 1946.

*Bibliotheca Bibliographica. Librorum Sedecimi Saeculi. Bibliographisches Repertorium für die Drucke des XVI Jahrhunderts.* Baden-Baden: Heitz, 1968.

Bohn, Henry George–see Lowndes' *The Bibliographer's Manual.*

Brunet, Jacques Charles. *Manuel du Libraire et de l'Amateur de Livres Contenant 1°. Un Nouveau Dictionnaire Bibliographique, 2°. Une Table en Forme de Catalogue Raisonné.* 6v. 5. éd. originale entièrement refondue et augm. d'un tiers par l'auteur. Paris: Firmin Didot Frères, Fils et Cie., 1860–63. Reprinted in Berlin by Atmann in 1922.
This descriptive catalogue also contains facsimiles of printers' marks, title-pages, etc., as well as an alphabetical list of books sold at auction.

Brunet, Jacques Charles. *Supplément, Contenant 1° Un Complèment du Dictionnaire Bibliographique. . . . 2° La Table Raisonnée des Articles au Nombre d'environ 10,000 décrits au Présent Supplément.* Par MM. P. Deschamp and G. Brunet. Paris: Dorbon-Aine, 1928.

Brunet, Jacques Charles. *Dictionnaire de Géographie Ancienne et Moderne à l'Usage du Libraire et de l'Amateur de Livres.* Par un bibliophile. Paris: Dorbon-Aine, 1928.

Brunet, Jacques Charles. *Table Alphabétique des Noms d'Auteurs et des Ouvrages Anonymes.* Paris: Potter, 1868.

Brunet, Jacques Charles. *Nouvelles Recherches Bibliographiques Pour Servir de Supplément au Manuel du Libraire et de l'Amateur de Livres.* 3v. Paris: Chez Silvestre, 1834.

Brunet's work superseded G. B. Bure's *Bibliographie Instructive.* Brunet, a senior librarian for the State, was a major force in French bibliographical circles. He lived from 1780 to 1867.

Gamba, Bartolomeo. *Serie dei Testi di Lingua e di Altre Opere Importanti nella Italiana Letteratura Scritte dal Sec. XIV al XIX.* IV ed. Venezia: co' tipi del Gondoliere, 1839.

Gesner, Konrad. *Bibliotheca Universalis siue Catalogus Omnium Scriptorum Locupletissimus, in Tribus Linguis, Latina, Graeca, & Hebraica: Extantium & Non Extaniŭ, ueterum & Recentiorum in hunc usq. diem Doctorum & Indoctorum, Publicatorum & in Bibliothecis Latentium. Opus Nouum, & nŏ Bibliothecis tantum Publicis Priuatisue Instituendis Necessarium, sed Studiosis Omnibus cuiuscunq/ue/ Artis aut Scientiâe ad Studia Melius Formanda Utilissimum.* Tiguri: Apud Christophorum Froschouerum 1545.

This work was published in Zürich by the author, a 16th century physician (1516–1565), who in the span of a few short years produced numerous works, including this early attempt at listing books published in Latin, Greek, Hebrew, etc.

Georgi, Theophilus (sometimes written Konrad Georgi, ca. 1674–1762). *Allgemeines Europäisches Bücher-Lexicon, in Welchem nach Ordnung des Dictionarii die Allgemeinen Autores odor Gattungen von Büchern zu Finden, Welche . . . noch vor dem Anfange des XVI. Seculi bis 1739 Inclusive . . . in dem Europäischen Theile der Welt, sondernlich aber in Teutschland, sind Geschrieben und Gedrucket Worden.* 5v. in 2. Leipzig.

Georgi, Theophilus. *Supplement . . . in welchem . . . die von 1739 bis / 1757/ inclus.* Neu-Edierten un Wieder Aufgelgeten Bücher zu Finden. 3v. Leipzig: W. H. Schöenermarck, 1758.

The five volumes cover the period 1501 to 1757, including all European authors.

Harvard College Library. *French Sixteenth-Century Books.* 2v. Cambridge, Mass.: Harvard University Press, 1964.

Harvard College Library. *Italian Sixteenth-Century Books.* 2v. Cambridge, Mass.: Harvard University Press, 1975.

Haym, Niccola Francesco. *Biblioteca Italian Ossia Notizia de' Libri Rari Italiani Divisa in Quattro Parti.* 4v. Milano: Silvestri, 1803.

*Index Aureliensis. Catalogus Librorum Sedecimo Saeculo Impressorum.* Baden-Baden: Heitz, 1962.

Lowndes, William Thomas. *The Bibliographer's Manual of English Literature Containing an Account of Rare, Curious and Useful Books, Published in or Relating to Great Britain and Ireland, From the Invention of Printing: with Bibliographical and Critical Notices, Collations of the Rarer Articles, and the Prices at Which They Have Been Sold.* New ed., rev., cor. and enl., with an Appendix Relating to the Books of the Literary and Scientific Societies, by Henry G. Bohn. London: Bell & Daldy, 1865.

Maclès, Louise-Noëlle. *Les Sources du Travail Bibliographique.* 19v. Genève-Lille: Droz-Giard, 1950.

This major work contains bibliographies of bibliographies, general bibliographies, the 15th and 16th centuries, catalogues published by libraries, national bibliographies, specialized bibliographies, historical bibliographies, etc. An essential reference work.

Martini, Giuseppi Sergio. *Italia Bibliographica.* Firenze: Sansoni Antiquariato, 1953-

*New Cambridge Bibliography of English Literature.* Cambridge: Cambridge University Press.

Ottino, Giuseppe, and Fumagolli, Giuseppe. *Bibliotheca Bibliographica Italica. Catalogo di Scritti di Bibliologia Bibliografia e Biblioteconomia Pubblicati in Italia e quelli Risguardanti l'Italia Pubblicati all'Estero.* 2v. Roma: Pasqualucci, 1889–1895.

Followed by several supplementary volumes, 1895–1902, covering most subject headings. This useful work was reprinted, with the supplementary volumes, at Graz: Akademische Druck-u. Verlagsanstalt, 1957.

Pagliaini, Attilio. *Catalego General della Libreria Italiani.* Milano: S.A.B.E., 1901-

Panzer, Georg W.F. *Annales Typographici ad Annum 1536.* 11v. 1793–1803.

Peddie, Robert A. *Subject Index of Books Published up to and Including 1880.* 4v. (A–Z). London: Grafton & Co., 1939.

Peddie published several smaller works on 15th century books, color printing, and place names, but the *Subject Index* remains his major opus.

Pollard, Alfred W., and Redgrave, G. R. A. *A Short-title Catalogue of Books Printed in England, Scotland and Ireland, and of English Books Abroad, 1475-1640.* London: The Bibliographical Society, 1926.

Ricci, Seymour de. *The Book Collector's Guide. A Practical handbook of British and American Bibliography.* Philadelphia, New York: The Rosenbach Co., 1921.

Sadleir, Michael. *XIX Century Fiction: A Bibliographical Record.* 2v. Cambridge: Cambridge University Press [1951].

Wing, Donald G. *A Short-title Catalogue of Books Printed in England, Scotland, Ireland, Wales and British America and of English Books Printed in Other Countries, 1641–1700.* 3v. 1945–51.

The second edition of this work appeared in 1972. This work continues that of Pollard and Redgrave.

Zambrini, Francesco. *Le Opere Volgari a Stampa dei Secoli XIII e XIV.* IV ed. Bologna: Zanichelli, 1884.

And the supplement to this by Salomone Morpurgo. *Le Opere Volgari . . . dei Secoli XIII et XIV Indicate e Descritte da F. Zambrini.* Bologna: Zanichelli, 1929.

## National Bibliographies

See the catalogs of the various national libraries, e.g., the Bibliothèque Nationale's *Catalogue Général des Livres Imprimes. Auteurs.* Paris: Imprimerie Nationale, 1897–; the British Museum's (Library's) numerous catalogs, including the *Catalogue of Printed Books.* 95v. London: Clowes, 1881–1900; the Library of Congress's *Catalogue of Books Represented by the Library of Congress,* 167v. Ann Arbor: Edward, 1942–1946, and of course the *National Union Catalogue;* the Biblioteca Nazionale Centrale–Firenze, *Bolletti delle Publicazioni Italiane, Ricevute per Diritto di Stampa.* Firenze: Biblioteca Nazionale Centrale, 1886–, and those of Rome, etc.

## INCUNABULA

Burger, Konrad. *The Printers and Publishers of the XV. Century, with Lists of Their Works: Index to the Supplement to Hain's Repertorium Bibliographicum* etc., in Part 2, Vol. 2 of Walter A. Copinger's *Supplement to Hain's Repertorium Bibligraphicum.* London: H. Sothern, 1902.

Burger, Konrad. *Supplement zu Hain und Panzer. Beiträge zur Inkunabelbibliographie. Nummerconcordanz von Panzers Lateinis-*

*chen und Deutschen Annalen und Ludwig Hains Repertorium Bibliographicum.* Leipzig: Hiersemann, 1908. Reprinted in 1966 by Olms at Hildesheim.

Copinger, Walter A. *A Supplement to Hain's Repertorium Bibliographicum: or Collections Towards a New Edition of that Work.* 2v. in 3. London: Sotheran, 1895–1902, and reprinted by Görlich Editore, in Milan in 1950.

This important work by the celebrated English bibliographer consists of two parts, the first containing nearly 7,000 corrections of and additions to the collations of works described or mentioned by Hain; the second, a list with numerous collations and bibliographical data of nearly 6,000 volumes printed in the fifteenth century omitted by Hain. There are also addenda to Parts I and II and an Index by Konrad Burger—see above. The works are listed alphabetically by author.

Hain, Ludwig F. T. *Repertorium Bibliographicum, in quo Libri Omnes ab Arte Typographica Inventa usque ad Annum M.D. Typis Expressi Ordine Alphabetico vel Simpliciter Enumeratur vel Adcuratius Recensentur.* 2v. in 4. Stuttgart: J. G. Cotta, 1826–1838, and reprinted by Görlich in Milan in 1948.

The first edition, comprising some 16,000 titles, served as the nucleus for all the above works (by Burger, Copinger, and then by Reichling), though the printing of that edition was small and smudged and frequently difficult to read.

Panzer, George Wolfgang Franz. *Annales Typographici, ab Artis Inventae Origine ad Annum 1500.* 5v. Nuremberg: Zeh, 1793–1797.

Panzer, Georg Wolfgang Franz. *Annales Typographici, ab Anno 1501 ad Annum 1536.* 6v. Nuremberg: Zeh, 1798–1803. These two works were reprinted by Olms at Hildesheim, 1963–1964, as 11 volumes. In their article on "Incunabula" in the *Encyclopedia of Library and Information Science,* Almagno and Immroth state—"This work is considered by some scholars the first important modern bibliography." The divisions are made alphabetically, listing the principal centers of printing, and then followed (under each city) by the printers and the chronological listing of their works, though Proctor later criticized some aspects of Panzer's approach to the subject.

Reichling, Dieterieux. *Appendices ad Hainnii-Copingeri Repertorium Bibliographicum Additiones et Emendationes Edidit.* 7v. in 3. Milan: Görlich Editore, 1953.

_____. *Svpplementvm (Maximam Partem e Bibliotheis Helvetiae*

*Collectvm) cvm indice vrbivm et Typographorvm. Accedit Index Avctorvm Generalis Totivs Operis.*
This is bound with volume two of Reichling's *Appendices* (above).

These works by Burger, Copinger, Hain, and Reichling constitute a single unit as a reference work, listing the works alphabetically by author. Although they do not include every work published in the fifteenth century, they refer to the vast majority; others are mentioned under Bibliographies in this chapter.

British Museum. *Catalogue of Books Printed in the XVth Century Now in the British Museum.* London: Printed by Order of the Trustees, 1902. See also, R. Proctor, below.

Duff, E. Gordon. *Fifteenth Century English Books: A Bibliography of Books and Documents Printed in England and of Books for the English Market Printed Abroad.* London: The Bibliographical Society, 1917.

*Gesamtkatalog der Wiegendrucke, Herausgegeben von der Kommission für den Gesamtkatalog der Wiegendrucke.* 8v. Leipzig: K.W. Hiersemann, 1925–1940.
See also Thomas Accurti's *Aliae Editiones Saeculi.*

Goff, Frederick. *Incunabula in American Libraries: A Third Census of Fifteenth-Century Books Recorded in North American Collections.* New York: Bibliographical Society of America, 1964.
This is the basic work on North American collections, though it is far from complete. It lists the authors and the variant author forms and contains an index of printers and publishers.

Guarnaschelli, T., Valenziani, E., and Cerulli, F. *Indice Generale degli Incunabuli delle Biblioteche d'Italia.* Roma: Istituto Poligr. dello Stato, 1943.
Refers to Incunabula in all Italian libraries, except those in the Vatican.
This important work is rarely cited by Anglo-American bibliographers.

Oates, J.C.T. *A Catalogue of the Fifteenth-Century Printed Books in the University Library.* Cambridge: Cambridge University Press, 1954.
Cambridge has a nearly perfect collection of British incunabula, and this work is most useful.

Pellechet, Marie L.C. *Catalogue Général des Incunables des Bibliothèques Publiques de France.* 3v. Paris: A. Picard et Fils, 1897–1909.

The author published several other works on printing societies and liturgical works, but this one still remains the basic reference work on French incunabula. Volumes 2 and 3 were continued by Louis Polain. See Polain for volumes 4–26, published in 1970 by photolithography.

Polain, Louis. *Catalogue des Livres Imprimés au Quinzième Siècle des Bibliothèques de Belgique.* 4v. Bruxelles: La Société des Bibliophiles & Iconophiles de Belgique, 1932.

It is curious that this important reference work is not cited more often. The works are listed alphabetically by author, and tables are included. Many of Belgium's incunabula were destroyed by German armies in the First World War.

Proctor, Robert. *An Index to the Early Printed Books in the British Museum: From the Invention of Printing to the Year 1500, with Notes of those in the Bodleian Library.* London: Holland Press, 1960, a reprint of the work originally published, 1898–1906.

Between Proctor and Oates, the English holdings are fairly well documented. Proctor of course followed the system of listing works first by country, then by town or city, and then by the press, chronologically. This system, that of the historical classification of books, was begun in the mid-nineteenth century by the Cambridge University Librarian, Henry Bradshaw, who developed this "natural-history method," i.e., according to their "genetic origin."

Stillwell, Margaret B. *Incunabula and Americana, 1450–1800. A Key to Bibliographical Study.* New York: Cooper Square Publishers, 1961.

Includes early works in Spanish.

Voulliéme, Ernst H. *Der Buchdruck Kölns bis zum Ende des Fünfzehnten Jahrhunderts. Ein Beitrag zur Inkunabelbibliographie.* Bonn: H. Behrendt, 1903.

Voulliéme, Ernst H. *Die Deutschen Drucker des Fünfzehnten Jahrhunderts.* Berlin: Reichsdruckerei, 1922.

Winship, George Parker, ed. *Census of Fifteenth Century Books Owned in America.* New York: The Bibliographical Society of America, 1919.

With author entries, prepared by the Bibliographical Society of America.

## PRINTING, TYPES, AND DEVICES

Aldis, Harry Gidney. *The Printed Book: The Original Manual Rev. and Brought up to Date by John Carter and Brooke Crutchey.* 3rd ed. Cambridge: Cambridge University Press, 1951.

Ames, Joseph. *Typographical Antiquities, or The History of Printing in England, Scotland, and Ireland.* 4v. Hildesheim: Georg Olms Verlagsbuchhandlung, 1969.

Originally published in 1749, this work contains illustrations and long biographical sketches of printers, e.g., Wm. Caxton (1st volume), Wynkyn de Worde, Richard Pynson, etc.

Berjeau, Jean Philibert. *Early Dutch, German, and English Printers' Marks.* London: E. Rascol, 1866–69.

This brief work contains 100 facsimiles, which were issued in parts over three years.

Bodoni, Giambattista. *Manuale Tipograficó.* 3v. Parma: Presso La Vedova, 1818.

Burger, Konrad. *Monumenta Germaniae et Italiae Typographica.* Berlin: O. Harrassowitz, 1892–1913.

Burger, Konrad. *Die Drucker und Verleger in Spanien und Portugal von 1501–1536.* Leipzig: K. W. Hiersemann, 1913.

Christian, M. A. *Origines de l'Imprimerie en France. Conférences Faites les 25 juillet et 17 août 1900.* Paris: Imprimerie Nationale, 1900.

Text, illustrations of printing and woodcuts.

Claudin, Anatole. *Antiquités Typographiques de la France.* 3v. Paris: A. Claudin, 1880–97.

Claudin, Anatole. *Histoire de l'Imprimerie en France au XVe et au XVIe Siècle.* 5v. Paris: Imprimerie Nationale, 1900–1915. Continued after 1926 by Seymour de Ricci in his *Documents sur la Typographie et la Gravure en France, aux XVe et XVIe Siècles, Réunis par A. Claudin, Publiés et Commentés par Seymour de Ricci.* London: Maggs Bros., 1926.

Claudin's work is essential to any reference section. Claudin was a most prolific writer, and produced a variety of catalogues, bibliographies, and histories of printing and binding, concentrating for the most part on the origins of printing in Auch, Franche-Comté, Guyenne, Hesdin-en-Artois, Languedoc, Limoges, Normandie, Paris, Provence, Reims, and Uzès.

Davies, Hugh William. *Devices of the Early Printers, 1457–1560. Their History and Development, with a Chapter on Portrait Figures of Printers*. London: Grafton & Co., 1935.
Some illustrations, useful.

*Deutscher Buchdruck im Jahrhundert Gutenbergs, zur Fünfthundert-Jahrfeier der Erfindung des Buchrucks. Herausgegeben von der Preussischen Staatsbibliothek und von der Gesellschaft für Typenkunde des 15. Jahrhunderts Wiegendruckgesellschaft.* Leipzig: Otto Harrossowitz, 1940.
Composed entirely of illustrations.

Duff, E. Gordon. *Early English Printing. A Series of Facsimilies of all the Types Used in England during the XVth Century with Some of Those Used in the Printing of English Books Abroad.* London: Kegan Paul, Trench, Trübner and Co., 1896.
Photographic plates of original works.

Enschedé, Charles. *Fonderies de Caractères et Leur Matériel dans les Pays-Bas du XVe au XIXe siècle.* Haarlem: E.F. Boh, 1908.

Feliu Cruz, Guillermo. *Bibliografia Histórica de la Imprenta en Santiago de Chile, 1818–1964.* Santiago, Chile: Talleres de la Editorial Nascimenta, 1964.

Haebler, Konrad. *Italian Incunabula.* Trans. by André Barbey. 3v. Munich: Weiss & Co., 1927. Includes two large unbound folio volumes of plates.

Haebler, Konrad. *The Early Printers of Spain and Portugal.* London: The Bibliographical Society, 1897.
Illustrated.

Haebler, Konrad. *Typenrepertorium der Wiegendrucke.* 5v. 3. Liechtenstein Nendeln; Wiesbaden: Kraus Reprints and Otto Harrossawitz, 1968.
Reprint of the work first published, 1905–1922.
Illustrated.

Heckethorn, Charles William. *The Printers of Basle in the XV and XVI Centuries, their Biographies, Printed Books and Devices.* London: Unwin Brothers, 1897.
Illustrations.

Hellinga, Wytze and Lotte. *The XVth Century Printing Types of the Low Countries.* 2v. Amsterdam: Menno Hertzberger, 1966.

Hellinger, W.G. *Copy and Print in the Netherlands, An Atlas of Historical Bibliography.*

Holtrop, Jan Willem. *Monuments Typographiques des Pays Bas au Quinzième Siècle; Collection de Fac-simile d' Après les Originaires Conservés à la Bibliothèque Royale de la Haye et Ailleurs.* La Haye: M. Nijhoff, 1857–1868.
Issued in parts over 11 years, this work includes block-books and printing.

Isaac, Frank. *English and Scottish Printing Types, 1501–1558.* 3v. Oxford: Oxford University Press, 1930–32.
Fully illustrated.

Johnson, John. *Typographia or the Printer's Instructor. Including an Account of the Origin of Printing, with Bibliographical Notices of the Printers of England, from Caston to the Close of the Sixteenth Century. A Series of Ancient and Modern Alphabets, and Domesday Characters. . . .* 2v. London: Longman, Hurst, Reese, Orme, Brown and Green. 1824.

McKerrow, Ronald B. *A Dictionary of Printers and Booksellers in England, Scotland and Ireland and of Foreign Printers of English Books, 1557–1640.* London: The Bibliographical Society, 1960.

McKerrow, Ronald B. *Printers & Publishers' Devices in England and Scotland, 1485–1640.* London: The Bibliographical Society, 1913.
Described, then fully illustrated.

Moran, James. *Printing Presses, History and Development from the Fifteenth Century to Modern Times.* Berkeley, Calif.: University of California Press, 1973.

Mores, Edward Rowe. *A Dissertation Upon English Typographical Founders and Founderies (1778), with a Catalogue and Specimen of the Type-foundry of John James (1782).* Oxford: Oxford Bibliographical Society, 1961.

Morison, Stanley. *Four Centuries of Fine Printing. Upwards of Six Hundred Examples of the Work of Presses Established during the Years 1500 to 1914.* London: Ernest Benn, Ltd. [1924]
Consists chiefly of plates of works published in Italy, France, Germany, Switzerland, the Low Countries, England, and some from the United States.

Morison, Stanley. *John Fell. The University Press and the 'Fell' Types. The Punches and Matrices Designed for Printing in the Greek, Latin, English, and Oriental Languages Bequested in 1686 to the University of Oxford.* Oxford: Clarendon Press, 1967.
Illustrations and plates.

Morison, Stanley, ed. *Type Specimen Facsimiles, Reproductions of Fifteen Specimen Sheets Issued Between the Sixteenth and Eighteenth Centuries.* 2v. London: Bowes & Bowes, Putnam, 1963.
Good, succinct historical notes, with a second loose leaf volume of plates.

Newberry Library. *Dictionary Catalogue of the History of Printing from the John M. Wing Foundation.* 6v. Chicago: G. K. Hall & Co, 1961.
A most useful work, but with numerous lacunae.

Panzer, George W. F. *Annales Typographici ad Annum 1536.* 11v.
A basic work on incunabula.

Peddie, Robert A., *Fifteenth Century Books. A Guide to Their Identification.* London: Grafton & Co., 1913.

Peddie, Robert A., ed. *Printing: A Short History of the Art.* London: Grafton & Co., 1927.

Plomer, Henry R. *English Printers' Ornaments.* London: Grafton & Co., 1924.
Last half of the book entirely illustrations.

Polain, Louis. *Marques des Imprimeurs et Libraires en France au XV Siècle.* Paris: Droz, 1926.

Pollard, Alfred W. *An Essay on Colophons, with Specimens and Translations.* New York: Burt Franklin, [n.d.]. A reprint of the 1905 publication.

Pollard, Alfred W. *Fine Books.* New York: G. P. Putnam, 1912.

Pottinger, David T. *The French Book Trade in the Ancien Régime, 1500–1791.*

Ricci, Seymour de. *Documents sur la Typographie et la Gravure en France.* This a continuation of Claudin's *Histoire* (see Claudin). De Ricci was a fine scholar who published a couple of dozen works including bibliographies and catalogues, covering a wide range of materials from incunabula to Aramaic Papyri. He was associated with Rosenbach for years.

Roberts, W. *Printers' Marks. A Chapter in the History of Typography.* London: George Bell & Sons, 1893.
A popular illustrated work.

Silver, Rollo G. *The American Printer, 1787–1825.* Charlottesville: Bibliographical Society of the University Press of Virginia, 1927.

Silver, Rollo G. *Type-founding in America, 1787–1825.* Charlottesville: Bibliographical Society of the University Press of Virginia, 1965.

Reed, Talbot Baines. *A History of the Old English Letter Foundries.*
London: Dawson, 1981.

Steinberg, Sigfrid H. *Five Hundred Years of Printing.* Har-
mondsworth, England: Penguin Books, 1953.
The most useful single volume work on the subject, with plates.

Thierry-Poux, Olgar. *Premiers Monuments de l'Imprimerie en France
au XVe Siècle.* Paris: Hachette, 1890.
A brief but knowledgeable account.

Thomas, Isaiah. *The History of Printing in America, with a Biography
of Printers & an Account of Newspapers.* Barre, Mass.: Imprint
Society, 1970. (First published in 1810.)
Too much under one hat, but an useful early work.

Updike, D. Berkeley. *Printing Types, Their History, Forms and Use.*
2v. 2nd edition. Cambridge, Mass.: Harvard University Press,
1932.
Still basic, with illustrations and plates.

Vervliet, H.D.L. *Sixteenth-century Printing Types of the Low
Countries.*

Winship, George Parker. *Gutenberg to Plantin. An Outline of the
Early History of Printing.* New York: B. Franklin Press, 1968.
A reprint of the 1926 Cambridge edition.

Wroth, Lawrence C., ed. *A History of the Printed Book.* New York: The
Limited Edition Club, 1938.
An illustrated work which covers every aspect of printing over the
centuries, though not all chapters are of equal depth and scholarship.


## BOOKBINDING

Abbey, J. R. *English Bindings, 1490–1940 in the Library of J.R. Abbey.*
Ed. by G. H. Hobson. London: Privately Printed at the Chiswick
Press, 1940.

Carter, John. *Binding Variants in English Publishing, 1820–1900.*
London: Constable & Co.: New York: R. Long and Richard R. Smith,
1932.
Illustrated.

Craig, Maurice. *Irish Bookbindings, 1600–1800.* London: Cassell, 1954.
A brief book, mostly plates.

Cundall, Joseph, ed. *On Bookbindings Ancient and Modern.* London: George Bell & Sons, 1881.

Cundall, Joseph. *On Ornamental Art Applied to Ancient and Modern Bookbinding.* London: Society of the Arts, 1948.

Davenport, Cyril J. H. *English Embroidered Bookbindings.* London: K. Paul, Trench, Trübner, 1899.

Davenport was the author of numerous other works on bookbindings.

Diehl, Edward T. *Bookbinding: Its Background and Techniques.* 2v. Port Washington, N.Y.: Kennikat Press, 1946.

*Fine Bindings, 1500–1700, from Oxford Libraries. Catalogue of Exhibitions.* Oxford: Bodleian Library, 1968.

Fletcher, William Younger. *Bookbinding in England and France. With Many Illustrations.* London: Seeley & Co., 1897.

Fournier, Edouard. *L'Art de la Reliure en France, aux Derniers Siècles.* Paris: E. Dentu, 1888.

With many illustrations.

Goldschmidt. E. Philip. *Gothic and Renaissance Bookbinding, Exemplified and Illustrated from the Author's Collection.* 2v. London: Ernest Benn, Ltd; Boston: Houghton Mifflin, 1928.

The second volume contains plates only. This work was reprinted in 1966.

Hodson, Geoffrey Dudley. *Blind-stamped Panels in the English Booktrade c. 1485–1555.* London: The Bibliographical Society, 1944.

Hobson, Geoffrey Dudley. *English Binding Before 1500.* Cambridge: Cambridge University Press, 1929.

Horne, Herbert P. *The Binding of Books, An Essay in the History of Gold-Tooled Bindings.* London: Kegan Paul, Trench, Trübner & Co., 1894. Republished by the Bibliographical Society in 1944.

McLean, Ruari. *Victorian Publishers' Bookbindings in Cloth and Leather.* Berkeley: University of California Press, 1973.

Marius, Michel. *La Reliure Française depuis l'Invention de l'Imprimerie Jusqu'à la Fin du XVIIIe Siècle.* Paris: D. Morgand, C. Fatout, 1888.

Matthews, Brandes. *Bookbindings Old and New. Notes of a Booklover with an Account of the Grolier Club of New York.* Illustrated. London and New York: MacMillan & Co., 1895.

Mejer, Wolfgang. *Bibliographie der Buchbinderei-Literatur.* Leipzig: Verlag Karl W. Hiersemann, 1925.

A useful work with references to much of Europe.

Middleton, Bernard C. *A History of English Craft Bookbinding Techniques.* New York: Hafner, 1963.
An excellent detailed technical study.

Needham. Paul. *Twelve Centuries of Bookbindings, 400–1600.* Oxford: Oxford University Press, 1979.

Nixon, Howard M. *Broxbourne Library, Styles and Designs of Bookbinding from the Twelfth to the Twentieth Century.* London: Maggs Bros., 1956.
Excellent, providing description of styles and history of designers and binderies. Good photographs, some color.

Nixon, Howard M. *English Restoration Bookbinding.* London: British Museum Publications, 1974.

Nixon, Howard M. *Five Centuries of English Bookbindings.* London: Scolar Press, 1978.

Pollard, Graham. "Changes in the Style of Book Binding, 1500–1830," *The Library,* XI (1956), 71–94.

Roquet, Antoine Ernest [Pseud. Ernest Thoinan] *Les Reliures Françaises (1500–1800). Biographie Critique et Anecdotique Précédées de l'Histoire de la Communauté des Relieurs et Doreurs de Livres de de la Ville de Paris et d'Une Etude sur les Styles de Relieurs.* 2v. Paris: E. E. Paul, L. Huard et Guillemin, 1893.
Although he was a prolific writer in the field of music, this was the author's primary work on bookbinding.

Sadleir, Michael. *The Evolution of Publishers' Binding Styles, 1770–1900.* London: Constable & Co.; New York: R.R. Smith, 1930.

Thoinan, Ernest. A pseudonym for A.E. Roquet, see under "Roquet."

Thomas, Henry. *Early Spanish Bookbindings XI–XV Centuries.* Oxford: The Bibliographical Society, 1939.

Zaehnsdorf, Joseph W. *The Art of Bookbinding, A Practical Treatise.* 2nd ed., revised & enlarged. Farnborough: Gregg, 1967.

## ENGRAVINGS, WOODCUTS, AND OTHER FORMS OF ILLUSTRATION

Beraldi, Henri. *Les Graveurs du XIXe Siècle–Guide de l'Amateur d'Estampes Modernes.* Paris: Librairie L. Conquest, 1885.

British Museum. *A Guide to the Processes and Schools of Engraving.* 3rd edition. London: W. Clower, 1933.

British Museum. *Schools of Illumination.* 6 Parts. London: Printed by Order of the Trustees, 1914–1930.

Courboin, François. *La Gravure en France, des Origines à 1900.* Paris: Delagrave, 1923.

Diringer, David. *The Illuminated Book: Its History and Production.* Rev. ed. New York: Praeger, 1967.
With numerous plates.

Davenport, Cyril J.H. *Mezzotints.* London: Methuen and Co., 1904.

Hamerton, Philip Gilbert. *Etching and Etchers.* Boston: Little, Brown, 1908.

Herbert, John Alexander. *Illuminated Manuscripts.* London: Methuen & Co., 1911.
Numerous plates.

Hind, Arthur M. *Engraving in England in the 16th and 17th Centuries. A Descriptive Catalogue.* 2v. Cambridge: Cambridge University Press, 1952.

Hind, Arthur M. *A History of Engraving and Etching from the 15th Century to the Year 1914.* New York: Dover Publications, 1923.

Hind, Arthur M. *An Introduction to a History of Woodcut, with a Detailed Survey of Work Done in the Fifteenth Century.* 2v. New York: Dover Publications, 1963.

Hofer, Philip. *Baroque Book Illustration. A Short Survey from the Collection in the Department of Graphic Arts, Harvard College Library.* Cambridge: Harvard University Press, 1970.

Linton, W. J. *A History of Wood-engraving in America.* New York: Longwood Press, 1977.
(First published in 1882.)

Loring, Rosamond B. *Decorated Book Papers, Being an Account of Their Designs and Fashions.* 2nd ed., edited by Philip Hofer. Cambridge, Mass.: Harvard University Press, 1952.

McClean, Ruari. *Victorian Book Design and Colour Printing.* 2nd ed. Berkeley and Los Angeles: University of California Press, 1972.

McKerrow, Ronald B., and Ferguson, F. S. *Title-page Borders Used in England and Scotland, 1485–1640.* London: Oxford University Press, 1935.
With numerous illustrations.

Ottley, William Young. *An Inquiry into the Origin and Early History of Engraving, upon Copper and in Wood, with an Account of Engravers and Their Works, from the Invention of Chalcogrophy by*

*Maso Finiguerra, to the Time of Marc' Antonio Raimondia.* 2v. London: J. and A. Arch, 1816.

This work is illustrated. Ottley's numerous books include the subjects of art, etchings, engravings, and a history of printing.

Pennell, Joseph, and Pennell, Elizabeth Robins. *Lithography & Lithographers. Some Chapters in the History of the Art.* New York: The Century Co.; London: T. Fisher Unwin, 1898.

Pollard, Alfred W. *Early Illustrated Books: A History of the Decoration and Illustration of Books in the 15th and 16th Centuries.* 2nd ed. New York: Haskell House, 1968.

Pollard was the author of several studies on illustrations and woodcuts in France, Italy, Venice, and England.

Prideaux, Sarah T. *Aquatint Engraving: A Chapter in the History of Book Illustration.* London: Duckworth, 1909.

Weber, Carl J. *Fore-edge Painting, A Historical Survey of A Curious Art in Book Decoration.* Irvington-on-Hudson, N.Y.: 1949.

Weber was known chiefly as a Thomas Hardy specialist.

Weber, Wilhelm. *A History of Lithography.* New York: McGraw Hill, 1966.

Most of the books in this section contain numerous illustrations and plates.


## PAPER AND WATERMARKS

Blum, André. *Les Origines du Papier de l'Imprimerie et de la Gravure.* Paris: Editeurs de la Tournelle, 1935.

Some of Blum's works have been translated into English.

Briquet, C. M. *Les Filigranes, Dictionnaire Historique des Marques du Papier, Dès Leur Apparition Vers 1282 Jusqu'en 1600.* 4v. 2ème édition. New York: Hacker Art Books, 1966.

A reprint of the 1923 edition. As impressive as this massive work is, the vast majority of watermarks still have not been traced and published in a single study.

Clapperton, Robert H., and Henderson, William. *Modern Papermaking.* 3rd edition. Oxford: Blackwell, 1952.

Hunter, Dard. *Primitive Papermaking.* Chillicothe, Ohio: Mountain House Press, 1927.

This book deals with the making and decorating of bark-paper. It contains both samples and illustrations.

Hunter, Dard. *Papermaking: The History and Techniques of an Ancient Craft.* 2nd ed. New York: Alfred Knopf, 1967.

Labarre, E. G. *Dictionary and Encyclopedia of Paper and Paper Making, with Equivalents of the Technical Terms in French, German, Dutch, Italian, Spanish and Swedish.* 2nd edition. Amsterdam: Swets & Zeitlinger, 1952.

Le Clert, Louis. *Le Papier à Troyes et aux Environs.* 2v. Paris: A l'Enseigne du Pégase, 1926.

Paper Publication Society. *Monumenta Chartae Papyraceae, or Collection of Works and Documents Illustrating the History of Paper.* This excellent series was edited by E. J. Labarre.

Vol. 1.   Heawood, Edward. *Watermarks, Mainly of Seventeenth and Eighteenth Centuries.* 1950.

2.   *The Briquet Album.* 1952.

3.   *Zonghi's Watermarks.* 1953.

4.   *Briquet's Opuscula.* 1955.

5.   *The Nostitz Papers.* 1956.

6.   Shorter, A. H. *Paper Mills and Paper Makers in England, 1495–1800.* 1957.

7.   Tscheidin, W. F. *The Ancient Paper Mills of Basle and Their Marks.* 1958.

8.   Eineder, G. *The Ancient Paper Mills of the Former AustroHungarian Empire and Their Watermarks,* 1960.

9.   Uchastkina, Z. V. *A History of Russian Hand Paper Mills and their Water-marks.* 1962.

10.   Lindt, J. *The Paper Mills of Berne and Their Watermarks.* 1964.

11.   *Tromonin's Watermark Album.* 1965.

12.   Subirà, Orio Valls I. *Paper and Watermarks in Catalonia.* 2v. 1970.

13.   Möslin, Vladimir. *Anchor Watermarks.* 1973.

Ris-Paquot, Oscard Edmond. *Dictionnaire Encyclopédique des Marques & Monogrammes, Chiffres, Lettres, Initiales, Signes, Figuratifs, etc.* 2v. Paris: Libraire Renouard, Henri Laurens, Editor, 1928.

Unfortunately this was the author's only excursion into this field, as all his other works deal chiefly with art.

## CONSERVATION AND PRESERVATION
## (INCLUDING MICROFORMS)

### Books

Banks, Paul A. *Treating Leather Bookbindings.* Chicago: The Newberry Library, 1974.

Barrow, William J. *The Barrow Method of Restoring Deteriorated Documents.* Richmond, Va.: W. J. Barrow Restoration Shop, 1973

Barrow, William J. *Manuscripts and Documents, Their Deterioration and Restoration.* Charlottesville, Va.: University Press of Virginia, 1972.

Barrow, William J. *Permanence/Durability of the Book.* Richmond, Va.: W. J. Barrow Laboratory.

Baumann, Roland M., ed. *Manual of Archival Techniques.* Harrisburg, Pa.: Pennsylvania Historical and Museum Commission, 1979.

Bohem, Hilda. *Disaster Prevention and Disaster Preparedness.* Office of Assistant Vice President—Library Plans and Policies, Systemwide Administration. Berkeley: University of California, 1978.

Clapp, Anne F. *Curatorial Care of Works of Art in Paper.* Rev. ed. Oberlin, Ohio: Intermuseum Conservation Association, 1973.

Cockerell, Douglas. *Bookbinding, and the Care of Books. A Text-Book for Bookbinders and Librarians.* London: Pitman & Sons, 1971.

Cunha, George M. and Dorothy G. *The Conservation of Library Materials.* 2v. Metuchen, N.J.: The Scarecrow Press, 1971.

Darling, Pamela W. *Preservation Planning Program: An Assisted Self-Study Manual for Libraries.* Washington, D.C.: Association of Research Libraries, Office of Management Studies, 1982.

Darling, Pamela W. *Preservation Planning Program Resource Notebook.* Washington, D.C.: Association of Research Libraries, Office of Management Studies, 1982. (1 volume, loose-leaf)

Greathouse, Glenn A., and Wessel, Carl J., eds. *Deterioriation of Materials, Causes and Preventive Techniques.* New York: Reinhold, 1954.

Guldbeck, P. *The Care of Historical Collections: A Conservation Handbook for the Nonspecialist.* Nashville: American Association for State and Local History, 1972.

Holmes, D. C. *Determination of the Environmental Conditions in a Library for the Effective Utilization of Microforms.* Washington, D.C.: Association of Research Libraries, 1970.

Horton, Caroline. *Cleaning and Preserving Bindings and Related Materials.* 2nd ed. Chicago: American Library Association, 1969.

Kane, Lucille M. *A Guide to the Care and Administration of Manuscripts.* Nashville: American Association for State and Local History, 1966.

Kathpalia, Y.P. *Conservation and Restoration of Archive Materials.* Paris: UNESCO, 1972.

Langwell, Harold. *The Conservation of Books and Documents.* London: Pitman & Sons, 1957.

Library of Congress. Entire series of publications and leaflets on preservation of leather bookbindings, archival material, etc.

Middleton, Bernard. *The Restoration of Leather Bindings.* Chicago: American Library Association, 1972. (Library Technology Program Publication No. 18).

Morrow, Carolyn Clarke. *Conservation Treatment Procedures: A Manual—Step-by-Step Procedures for the Maintenance and Repair of Library Materials.* Littleton, Colo.: Libraries Unlimited, 1982.

Morrow, Carolyn Clarke, and Schoenly, Steven B. *A Conservation Bibliography for Librarians, Archivists and Administrators.* Troy, N.Y.: Whitston Pub. Co., 1979.

Minogue, Adelaide. *The Repair and Preservation of Records.* Bulletin No. 5. Washington, D.C.: National Archives, 1943.

Santen, Vernon, and Crocker, Howard W. *Historical Society Records: Guidelines for a Protection Program.* Nashville: American Association for State and Local History, 1972. (Technical Leaflet No. 18).

Swartzburg, Susan G. *Preserving Library Materials. A Manual.* Metuchen, N.J.: The Scarecrow Press, 1980.

Wardle, D. B. *Document Repair.* London: Society for Archivists, 1971.

Waters, Peter. *Procedures for Salvage of Water-Damaged Library Materials.* Washington, D.C.: Library of Congress Press, 1975.

Winger, Howard W., and Smith, Richard D. *Deterioration and Preservation of Library Materials.* Chicago: University of Chicago Press, 1970.

Articles and Pamphlets

Banks, Paul N. "Paper Cleaning," *Restaurator,* I, No. 1 (1969), 52–66.

Blunn, Denis, and Petherbridge, Guy. "Leaf-Casting: Research into its Restoration and Conservation," *The Paper Conservator,* I (1977), 26.

Burdett, Eric. "Repairs to Books," in *The Craft of Bookbinding: A Practical Handbook.* London: David and Charles, 1975.

Clapp, Verner W. "The Story of Permanent/Durable Book-paper, 1115-1970," *Restaurator,* Supplement No. 3 (1972).

"The Cleaning of Prints, Drawings and Manuscripts on Paper: Dry Methods," one of several Conservation Information Program Slide Presentations available through Office of Museum Programs, Smithsonian Institution, Washington, D.C.

"Conserving Local Archival Materials on a Limited Budget." Technical Leaflet 86. *History News,* 30, No. 11 (Nov. 1975). American Association for State and Local History.

"Disposal of Microfilmed Records, Microfilm Storage and Filming Standards. Criteria for Using Microfilm Copies. Microfilm Services Available from GSA," *Federal Register,* 37 (Feb. 10, 1977), 2962-64.

Feller, Robert L. "Thermochemically Activated Oxidation: Mother Nature's Book Burning," *PLA Bulletin,* 28, No. 6 (1973), 232-42.

Greenfield, Jane. "No. 1, Wraparounds," "No. 2, Tip-ins & Pockets," "No. 3, Paper Treatment," "No. 4, Pamphlet Binding," "No. 5, The Small Bindery," 1980-1981. Some 14 pamphlets in this series have now been issued by: Preservation Office, Yale University.

Greenfield, Mary E. "Mylar Envelopes," *Guild of Book Workers Journal,* XI, No. 3 (Spring 1973), revised, 1979.

Gunner, Jean. *Simple Repair and Preservation Techniques for Collection Curators, Librarians and Archivists.* 2nd ed. Pittsburgh: Hunt Institute for Botanical Documentation, 1981.

"Halogenated Extinguishing Agent Systems," NFPA Pamphlet No. 12A. Boston: National Fire Protection Association, 1970.

Harris, Carolyn. "Mass Deacidification," *Library Journal* (July 1979), 1420-22.

Hey, Margaret, and Waters, Peter. "Heat-set Tissue Preparation and Application," Library of Congress Publication on Conservation of Library Materials. Conservation Workshop Notes. Series 300 No. 1, May 1977.

Hey, Margaret, and Waters, Peter. "Paper Bleachings: Its Simple Chemistry and Working Procedures," *The Paper Conservator,* 2 (1973), 10-23.

Indicator, N., et al. "An Evaluation of Pastes for Use in Paper Conservation," *Restaurator,* 2, No. 2 (1975), 139–50.

McAusland, Jane. "Facsimile Paper Repairs for Work of Art on Paper," *The Paper Conservator,* 3 (1978), 28–32.

Poole, Frazer G. "The Physical Protection of Brittle and Deteriorating Documents," *Library Science,* 5, No. 2 (June 1976), 9–11.

"Protection of Museum Collections: 1974," NFPA Pamphlet No. 911. Boston: National Fire Protection Association, 1974.

Segal, Judith, and Cooper, David. "The Use of Enzymes to Release Adhesives," *The Paper Conservator,* 2 (1977), 47–50.

Smith, David. "New Approaches to Preservation," *Library Quarterly,* 40 (Jan. 1970), 139–71.

Spawn, William. "Physical Care of Books and Manuscripts" in Jean Peters' *Book Collecting, A Modern Guide.* (New York: R. R. Bowker, 1977).

Tribolet, Harold W. "Rare Book and Paper Repair Techniques," *History News,* 25, No. 3 (March 1970). AASLH Technical Leaflet 13.

Weidner, Marilyn Kemp. "Damage and Deterioration of Art on Paper Due to Ignorance and the Use of Faulty Materials," *Studies in Conservation,* 12, No. 1 (1967), 5–25.

Microfilm

Bouscher, H. "Microforms: Can They Save our Treasures?" *Journal of Micrographics,* 7 (Jan.–Feb. 1974), 119–22.

Darling, Pamela W. "Developing a Preservation Microfilming Program," *Library Journal,* 99, 19 (Nov. 1, 1974), 2803–809.

Darling, Pamela W. "Microforms in Libraries: Preservation and Storage," *Microform Review* 5, No. 2 (April 1976), 93–100.

Diaz, A. J. "Microform Information Sources: Publications and Hardware," *Microform Review,* 4 (Oct. 1975), 350–61.

Hopler, F. B. "Micrographics: Processing, Storage and Protection," *Records Management Quarterly,* 10 (April 1976), 34–38.

Leisinger, A. H. "International Process in Microfilming: The Back-Ground and Work of the ICA Microfilm Committee," *American Archivist,* 39 (July 1976), 329–37.

Leisinger, A. H. "More on Permanence," *Microform Review* 4 (April 1975), 91–99.

Leisinger, A. H. "Microphotography for Archives." Washington, D.C. International Council on Archives, 1968.

Leisinger, A. H. "A Study of the Basic Standards for Equipping, Maintaining, and Operating a Reprographic Laboratory in Archives." Brussels: International Council for Archives, 1973.

Lynden, Frederick C. "Replacement of Hard Copy by Microforms," *Microform Review* 4, No. 1 (Jan. 1974), 15–23.

Rice, E. Stevens, and Dettling, Heinz. *Fiche and Reel: A Guide to Microfilm and Its Use.* 4th ed. Ann Arbor, Mich.: University Microforms International, 1980.

Sajor, Ladd Z. "Preservation Microfilming: Why, What, When, Who, How," *Special Libraries* 63, No. 4 (April 1972), 195–201.

Spaulding, Carl M. "Kicking the Silver Habit: Confessions of A Former Addict," and also the author's article, "On Spaulding's Diagnoses: Some Second Opinions," *American Libraries* 9, No. 11 (Dec. 1978), 665–69.

Veaner, Allen B. "Microreproduction and Micropublication Technical Standards: What They Mean to You, The User," *Microform Review* 3, No. 2 (April 1974), 80–84.


## BOOK AND MANUSCRIPT EVALUATION

*American Book Prices Current.* Published by Bancroft-Parkman, 1895–

*Book Auction Records,* published by Parke-Bernet Galleries, 1902–

*Bookman's Price Index.* A Guide to the Values of Rare and Other Out-of-Print Books. Completed by Daniel F. McGrath, 1964–

Bradley, Van Allen. *The Book Collector's Handbook of Values.* 3rd ed. New York: G. P. Putnam, 1978.

Howes, Wright. *U.S.-iana, 1650–1950.* New York: R. R. Bowker, 1962. On rare first American editions.

Johnson, Merle D. *Merle Johnson's American First Editions.* New York: R. R. Bowker, 1942.

Mandeville, Mildred S. *The Used Book Price Guide: Five-Year Edition.* Kenmore, Wash.: Price Guide Publishers, 1983.


## SOME JOURNALS PERTAINING TO RARE BOOKS, MANUSCRIPTS, ARCHIVES, AND THEIR ADMINISTRATION

*American Antiquarian Society Newsletter.* 185 Salisbury St., Worcester, MA 01609

*American Archivist.* Society of American Archivists, 801 S. Morgan, Chicago, IL 60680.

*American Book Collector,* Antiquarian Bookselling, Collecting & Bibliography. A commercial publication. 1434 S. Yale Ave., Arlington Heights, IL 60005

*Antiquarian Bookman* (The Specialist Book Trade Weekly). Box 1100, Newark, NJ 07101.

*Archives.* Published by the British Records Association, Master's Court, The Charterhouse, Charterhouse Square, London, EC1M 6AU. 1949, England

*Archives and Manuscripts* (Journal of the Australian Society of Archivists). Executive Director, Library Association of Australia, Box M222, Sydney Mail Exchange, N.S.W. 2012, Australia

*Archivum, International Review on Archives.* In French and English. Verlag Dokumentation, München, West Germany, 1951–.

*La Bibliofilia—Rivista di Storia del Libro e di Bibliografia.* Excellent articles in several languages. Casa Editrice Leo S. Olschki, Viuzzo del Pozzetto (Viale Europa), Caella Postale, 66, 50100 Firenze, Italia

*The Book Collector.* 3 Bloomsbury Place, London, WC1A 2QA, England

*Conservation Administration News.* University of Wyoming Libraries, Laramie, 1979– .

*Factotum.* Articles on computers, rare books, etc. Published by the British Library, Great Russell St., London, WC1B 3DG, England. 1978– .

*Fine Print, A Review of the Art of the Book.* Box 7741, San Francisco, CA 94120

*The Paper Conservateur.* Published by the Institute of Paper Conservation, London, 1976– .

*Penrose Annual; Review of the Graphic Arts.* Now published by Northwood Publications, Elm House, 10–16 Elm St., London, WC1A OBP, England 1896– .

*Restaurator,* For the Preservation of Library, Archival Matter. Excellent but often very technical. Munksgaard, Noerre Soegade 35, DK-1370 Copenhagen, K, Denmark

*UNESCO Journal of Information Science and Archives Administration,* formerly, UNESCO Bulletin for Libraries. UNESCO, 7–9 Place de Fonteney, 75700 Paris, France

*Scriptorium. Revue Internationale des Etudes Relatives aux Manuscrits.* Anvers, 1946– .

## PALEOGRAPHY

### Manuals

Barone, Nicola. *Paleografia Latina, Diplomatica e Nozioni di Scienze Ausiliarie.* 3a ed. Napoli: Rondinella & Loffredo, 1923.

Boeckler, Albert. *Abendländische Miniaturen bis zum Ausgang der Romanischen Zeit.* Berlin and Leipzig: [Teubner?] 1930.

Brandi, Karl. *Unsere Schrift. Drei Abhandlungen zur Einführung in die Geschicte der Schrift und des Buchdrucks.* Göttingen: Vandenhoeck & Ruprecht, 1911.

Bretholz, Berthold. *Lateinische Paläographie.* 3rd ed. Berlin and Leipzig: B. G. Teubner, 1926.

Floriano y Cumbreño, Antonio Cristino. *Curso General de Paleografí y Diplomática Españolas.* 2v. Oviedo: [Imprenta La Cruz], 1946

Garcia Villada, Zacarías. *Paleografía Española, precedida de una Introducción Sobre la Paleografía Latina e ilustrada con Veintinueve grabados. . . .* Madrid: [Revista de Filologia Española], 1923.

Lehmann, Paul Joachim Georg. *Lateinische Paläographie bis zum Siege der Karolingishen Minuskel.* Berlin and Leipzig: Teubner, 1925.

Madan, Falconer. *Medieval Palaeography.* Oxford: Clarendon Press, 1907.

Millares Corolo, Augustin. *Tratado de Paleografía Española.* Madrid: Hernando, 1932.

Muñoz y Rivero, Jesús. *Manual de Paleografía Diplomática Española de los Siglos XII al XVII. . . .* 2a ed. Madrid: Daniel Jorro, 1917.

Muñoz y Rivero, Jesús. *Paleografía Visigoda. Método teórico-practico para Apprender á Leer los Códices y Documentos Españoles de los Siglos V al XIII.* Nueva tirada. Madrid: D. Jorro, 1919.

Paoli, Cesare. *Grundriss zu Vorlesunger über Lateinische Palaeographie und Urkundelehre.* Aus dem italienischen Uebersetzt von Dr. Karl Lohmeyer. 3 parts in 1 vol. Innsbruck: Wagner, 1895–1902.

Paoli, Cesare. *Programma Scolastico di Paleografia Latina e di Diplomatica.* 3v. Firenze: G. C. Sansoni, 1901.

Prou, Maurice. *Manuel de Paléographie Latine et Française.* 4ème ed. Refon due avec la collaboration de Alain de Boüard: Paris: A. Picard, 1924.

Reusens, Edmond Henri Joseph. *Eléments de Paléographie.* Louvain: Chez l'Auteur, 1899.

Saunders, William. *Ancient Handwritings; An Introductory Manual for Intending Students of Palaeography and Diplomatic.* Walton-on-Thames: C.A. Bernau, 1909.

Thompson, Edward Maunde. *Handbook of Greek and Latin Palaeography.* 3rd ed. London: K. Paul, Trench, Trübner & Co., Ltd., 1906.

Vittani, Giovanni. *Nozioni Elementari di Paleografia e Diplomatic Milano: 1930.*

Wattenbach, Wilhelm. *Anleitung zur Lateinischen Palaeographie.* Leipzig: S. Hirzel, 1886.

Most of these authors have produced numerous other works on the subject of paleography which should be consulted as well. These manuals are always aided by collections of facsimiles and related subjects and the following have made outstanding contributions in this field: Auguste Bastard, John M. Burnam, Francesco Carta, Carlo Cipolla, Emile Chatelain, Anton Chroust, Hermann Degering, Ludovico Frati, Georg Leidinger, Elias Avery Lowe, Edward Maunde Thompson, Girolamo Vitelli, and George Frederic Warner.

# Index